FINDING A LEG TO STAND ON

Connie Bensley was born in south-west London, and has always lived there, apart from wartime evacuation. Until her retirement she worked as a secretary to doctors and to an MP and as a medical copywriter. Her latest book from Bloodaxe is *Finding a Leg to Stand On: New & Selected Poems* (2012), which presents new work with poems drawn from six previous collections: *Progress Report* and *Moving In*, originally published by Peterloo Poets, and four later books published by Bloodaxe: *Central Reservations* (1990), *Choosing To Be a Swan* (1994), *The Back and the Front of It* (2000) and *Private Pleasures* (2007).

CONNIE BENSLEY

FINDING A LEG TO STAND ON

NEW & SELECTED POEMS

BLOODAXE BOOKS

ISBN: 978 1 85224 956 4

First published 2012 by
Bloodaxe Books Ltd,
Highgreen,
Tarset,
Northumberland NE48 1RP.

www.bloodaxebooks.com
For further information about Bloodaxe titles
please visit our website or write to
the above address for a catalogue.

Supported using public funding by
ARTS COUNCIL
ENGLAND

Cover design: Neil Astley & Pamela Robertson-Pearce.

Printed in Great Britain by
Bell & Bain Limited, Glasgow, Scotland.

for Harriet, Catherine, Tom, Iona, Violet

ACKNOWLEDGEMENTS

This edition includes poems selected from these books by Connie Bensley: *Central Reservations: New & Selected Poems* (1990), *Choosing To Be a Swan* (1994), *The Back and the Front of It* (2000) and *Private Pleasures* (2007), all published by Bloodaxe Books. *Central Reservations* included poems from two earlier collections originally published by Peterloo Poets, *Progress Report* (1981) and *Moving In* (1984).

Acknowledgements are due to the editors of the following publications in which some of the new poems in the *Finding a Leg to Stand On* (2012) section of the book first appeared: *Acumen, The North, Orbis, The Poetry Paper, Poetry Review, The Reader, The Rialto, Smiths Knoll* and *The Spectator*.

CONTENTS

FROM

Progress Report

(1981)

Annual Dinner

I have sat here at this table now for years.
I have a race memory of this place;
Its formal flora, face-distorting spoons,
And the indigenous tribes, of bearers and borers.

Sometimes I dance, held hot against black serge,
And often I ask,
Shouting above the music,
About Croydon, or the Common Market, or the children.

Before the dancing we had the speeches,
And that was a peaceful time.
An interval of pleasant stupefaction
Infused with coffee and brandy.

Further back still, there was the cream gâteau
And, penetrating deeper layers of the past,
The lamb, the trout, the soup,
And, with each, a subject briskly explored,
To right and to left,
With eye contact and ego projection.

In the prehistoric, previous world
I was still here,
Empty and chattering over gin,
And smiling winningly into unfamiliar faces.

But, unlike some younger people,
I can still remember the world outside,
And I know that one day we will all go home
And find rest, and the cat waiting to be fed.

April

Here comes Spring.
Season (stirring dull blood) of spots
And suicides.
Better, those of us who are at risk
To skip April, May,
Miss the worst of the disorientation,
The conviction that life
Is coming up with some colossal romantic musical
For which the casting director has, yet again,
Overlooked you.

The hard light, the sudden knife-like breeze,
The grey pallor of those strips of skin
So tentatively bared.
The tender vulnerability of the pale buds in the hedge.

Dig up the garden
And stop your mind with your transistor.
This dangerous change will soon pass.

Cardiac Department

Discrete, disconsolate,
The heart patients gather in the waiting-room.
Drawn together, but facing apart
And thinking about their ECGs.

They'd like to pretend
They're in the buffet at King's Cross
Waiting for the 6.15:
But more serious matters are at stake:
Life insurance; or life itself.

The nurse is their mother here,
Her smiles flow out
Bright and inexhaustible as conjurors' bunting.

The cleaner is having a mysterious mid-morning clean.
'Don't move love,' she says,
'Don't move. I can dust round you.'

Comfort

In a meadow, redolent of summer,
Deep in green, each leaf gilded
Against the sky, sit three women
Smiling at the camera. They are fat
Beyond the merely Rubenesque.

Corseted in folding chairs,
Armoured in synthetics;
Their considerable legs stretch forward in unison.
In the East, they would be collectors' pieces.

One has a striped umbrella
Over her head. She suffers with the sun.
Another has the thermos, which she's handing on to Flo,
For Flo gets parched; and all of them are kind.

Indeed, if you were lost – if you had missed the path
That led back round the hill
They'd help you; they would hem you in
And wall you round with helpfulness.

Such a stockade:
No harm could penetrate.
You'd be safe there,
Safe, and in clover.

Commuter

Coke tins glisten in the showery gutters,
The turd-strewn grass is springing rank and green.
Dull glass catches light it had forgotten
And I am expected home on the six-fifteen,

In the warmth, my briefcase is relaxing;
The non-press collar manacles my neck.
Steam is rising from my pinstripe suiting,
I feel the message, but can I answer back?

My hand on the telephone is winter white.
It clams to the plastic. No one answers my call.
What can I do but order stones and piping,
Get to my garden, build a waterfall?

Crossing London to Suffolk

After the roadworks,
After the plastic shops and dusty gutters,
The tombstone flats rooted in concrete.

After the scrawled walls,
The town-grey faces,
The hard-edge brick and metalwork

Comes the first field:
Gold – tiger-striped
Where the stubble has been burned,

Blue pulled right down behind it:
Set and enmeshed
In cool green places,

Dreamed up by the inward urban eye
For summer. Yet in winter,
Under pewter light,

The neon shops and claustrophobic streets
Will pull me back to warmth and ugliness;
Home again, like a cat to the cupboard it knows.

Desires

Newly shaven, your eyes only slightly bloodshot,
Your rat-trap mouth smiling up at the corners,
You remind me of the Head Girl
I used to be in love with.

It's something about your sporty build,
The way you seem to be counting the people in the café
With a view to lining them up in teams.

It's quite set me in the mood for the evening,
And I follow you alertly through the door,
Hoping you'll turn and snap at me
To pick my feet up, and not to slouch.

Dig

Music, raucous behind the bushes,
Drew me into the graveyard.

A man was digging for the next incumbent,
Down to his elbows, his trannie by his side.

Man and bird, and Presley,
Raised their voices to heaven.

'You need a bit of a song,' said the man,
'When you're working to a deadline.'

Dropping Out

I planned to write this thesis, you see,
On cooking and personality –

You know the sort of thing:
The exhibitionist who flambés at table,
The introvert, who hides his food in pastry,
The impulsive griller,
The contemplative casseroler,
And the rigid, repressed personality
Who has to have each ingredient
Down to the last grain.

Unfortunately I overdid the practical work:
Became immersed in my theories,
Testing, tasting – wasting my spirit
In a lust for pasta,
Becoming, at last, a compulsive eater.

'You're trying to fill a void,' they said,
And sent me up to the Tavistock.

But somehow my problems made the analyst hungry.
We took to cooking ourselves bijou meals
And lying down to discuss them,
Whiling away whole nights
In psychogastric speculation.

That man has really taught me a thing or two,
And his light touch with a soufflé
Has quite made me forget my academic career.

The Emigré

What land is that, stained out
Across the wall?
I think I knew it when I was a boy.

Twisting my neck on the pillow
I can see the coast,
And that inlet – the grey shading into the shallows –
Where the village was.

My mother wore blue serge
Down to her boots.
The yard had a sunflower, so high
It looked in at my window.

There is the river where I used to fish
And never thought of time.

Here, all our time's paid out in tiny sips
And clocked by pills, and wiped away with gauze.

Yesterday they propped me up in bed.
Tomorrow I may get across the room
And see it all, once more.

Evidence

*'It is alleged that the incident took place
during a holiday in France.'*

Did intimacy take place?
Difficult to be sure.

Hands whispered over sunwarmed skin.
Murmurs, through tangled hair,
Were fervid. There was, perhaps –
Can one recall –
Some interpenetration of the flesh
In the shafting half-light from the afternoon blinds.

Movements and time were mindless;
Half-entranced by the clock's tick
And the clip of the blown vines
On the trellis wall.

But was there a world outside?
Or was it a room that was traced in the sand
(Where the incoming tide lapped a regular pulse)
By the hand of the dreamer, who seemed in his sleep
To feel salt lips on his closed eyes
In the dim room, with the clock's tick
And the tap of the vines in the faint breeze
From the warm sea
As it sighed, outside.

Father Christmas

Last year's Father Christmas
Caught pneumonia and died
Through standing in the shopping precinct
Shaking his tin in all weathers
Under the municipal Christmas tree.

This year's Father Christmas is of wax,
Sitting on a stool, apple-cheeked
And smiling without relief,
His tin intimately lodged between his knees.

He watches the lights change
(Green to amber, amber to red)
With bland accord.
It is the nature of things.

Yesterday someone fell under wheels
Before his very eyes,
Crying out, and bleeding in a Christmassy colour;
And he smiled and smiled,
Never turning his head at the ambulance bell
Or envying the attentions of the crowd.

February

February, a poor month for the foot fetishist:
Wellingtons, old clodhoppers,
Socks that have almost breathed their last,
And when the occasional foot is glimpsed, naked,
By the determined voyeur,
It is deathly pale and flabby,
Contoured and moulded by the winter boot,

And, though fascinating, hardly contemporary:
More like something unearthed from a previous season.

But dream hotly, you fellow fetishists
Of a spell in March,
When the weather may break, and evoke
The first disturbing sandals of the year.

God's Christmas Jokes

Christmas: there was the usual crop of disasters:
Planes, coaches, crashed.
(So often the victims are pilgrims
Or those on errands of mercy.)

In the home, the disasters are on a less heroic scale,
The stressful, claustrophobic press
Of one's nearest and dearest
Being by far the worst.

The snappy rejoinders, early on suppressed,
And by Day Three not suppressed.
The bathroom used for a quick fit of sobbing
And phone calls late at night
From suicidal single friends
Who have missed out on Perfect Love at Christmas.

On the first day after Bank Holiday the Sales begin,
And people shoot out from their doors like prisoners released,
Glad to be finished with their attempts at Peace on Earth
And bursting with meaty energy for the fray.

Hiatus

Ragworn with our emotions, out of sight
Of reason; ash-trays brimming by the bed,
We drag on through the fitful, racked-out night
Reiterating all that we have said
Ten times or more before, and still it fails
To lead us from the maze.
                              At last the dawn
Prefigures some release. The window pales.
I rest my head against it. On the lawn
I see the starlings quarrel, strut and jerk,
(Like some old newsreel, grainy black and grey),
Their energies close-channelled to their work:
Survival. Well they manage, so we may:
The day will come, and like awaited rain,
Will make our lives move forward once again.

Life Study

Dawn or dusk may find me,
Pressed well back into the landscape,
Crumbs in hand.

The stealth, the immobility, the bone-aching patience
Come easily to me.

So what chance do you have?
I have marked you down.
No force is necessary, except in my mind;
And slowly, by my graduated rewards,
You will come to my hand.

26

March

That night, the wind caught in the drainpipe,
Howling in tongues,
Frightening him upright in the bed.

The garbled message sent his heart wild to help –
Squeezing, jetting, damming,
Gushing, syncopating, fibrillating,
And finally cancelling itself out.

'How nice for him,' they said, at daybreak,
'To slip away quietly in his sleep.'

May

They're cutting grass below in Lincoln's Inn,
And by her desk, soft air is drifting in
With hints of lilac. Seven hours to go
Between these walls. 'Dear Sir,' the hours begin.

'Dear Sir,... My dearest Sir,' her fingers say
(With carbon copies) 'write to me today,
And tell me what you look like, who you are,
And if you feel the summer on its way.'

1915

Those mothers: how could they bear it?
Did they tear up the yellowing snapshots:

That picnic when he fell into the pond;
The outing with the Sunday school
(Scowling, mutinous, in the second row);
The cricket match; more groups, and last of all,
His first leave.
              He's almost finished, here,
With childish things.

Fresh-faced, wide-eyed he turns. He's on his way
To the muddy abattoir.

Lucky for us, whose children survive to mortgages
And greyness.

Parent and Child

See the parent and the child
Tossed by tides.

We try to tread rational waters,
But something darker closes over our heads,
Sweeping us apart and dashing us together.

Words cannot explain: they fuse with the wind,
Leaving the faces naked, the arms waving.

Sometimes a body is beached, gasping.

Turn it over with your foot.
One side is white, the other side is black.

Permissive Society

Wake, for the dawn has put the stars to flight,
    And in my bed a stranger: so once more,
What seemed to be a good idea last night
    Appears, this morning, sober, rather poor.

Provence

Provence, a name like perfumed air,
Warm fruit, herbs fragrant underfoot,
Emerald lizards,
And the sun, the sun,
Hot but not punishing:
Enough to dry the silver swimmer's skin
Before he pours the wine into his glass.

The small hotel, though vaguely picturesque,
Was dark, and had a queasy smell inside.
It wasn't quite as in the Michelin Guide.
The beds weren't made. Nobody at the desk.

Along the river banks the dream comes right,
But first you have to park your baking car.
They charge a lot. The heat dissolves the tar.
But then you see the swallowtails in flight
And if you walk on in the sweating sun,
The other, dreamed Provence, will have begun.

Recluse

This house is becoming inappropriate.
I am shrinking out of it:
Rattle about like a pea in a casket.

It used to fit me:
Now my voice echoes thinly in the corridors,
And lamplight fades out
Before it reaches the cold walls.

It used to be an ordinary size:
Now I sit uneasily in its cavern mouth,
Crouch in cupboards,
Move only with my back to the skirting-board.

Once somebody knocked,
But even in those days I could not reach the keyhole
To see who was there.

The Stable Relationship

Hatch in that hinterland
Which borders love and emptiness,
And that is where we live and move
And have our being.

Refugees from a warmer country,
We have no easy route back:
It is not in our gift.

A Suitable Case for Treatment

The transient and disparate forces that disrupt
the heart's rhythms can be treated.

DR KLEIN (Boston University)

Something is happening down in my pacemaker,
Something is stirring, alarming, divine,
Transient, lovely and disparate forces
Have entered my heart since your elbow touched mine.

Come and sit here and I'll show you my ECG:
My cardiologist thinks it looks fine:
But disparate forces need desperate courses,
So fly me please, darling, to see Dr Klein.

Synopsis

The lines are down between us. It's no use
To shout. We may as well
Add up the gain and loss,
Rule off the entry, and get out.

Or shall we try a new scenario?
The man preoccupied but equable;
The woman calm, but otherwise engaged,
And both of them placating, kind and fair?

Scratch under the veneer: there's more veneer.
We touched wood once, but it's no longer there.
Cry *sauve qui peut*:
New readers, start from here.

31

Technique

Life, you know, is set up by this great random computer
But it has been poorly programmed.
Someone has fed in more bad news than good,
And the messages tick out mad irrelevancies and ironies

Those putting in a modest request for comedy
Get tragedy, *tout court*:
And those banking on a touch of gravitas
Get the pratfall and the cauliflower ear.

It's no use fighting the system.
Keep a low profile, I say,
And if the messages come tapping out too black,
You can always go to earth.

Time Slip

When she left him, time would not move on.
It hung around him, stale as city air,
Inert, refusing to get the day over.

Chores, reflections, ruses, rituals,
All failed to budge this trick of time.
He shook the clock and studied the sun.

The day had fallen into a fault,
And there he turned, suspended,
At odds: beating at the vacuum,
Shouting for a hand to pull him back
Into chronology.

Travelling Light

This whiskery old dog shed its gaze over me,
Worshipping with brown and clouded eyes,
Thinking I was God knows what:
Saviour, provider, Second Comer, dog's delight.

He was putting on the limping walk,
Currying not only favour
But commitment, love, warmth –
Who knows what package of trouble?
Soliciting, and too old for it.

I pulled back, called a halt to the affair,
Turned off round a corner, put space behind me.

I like to travel light;
And yet all day I felt trammelled:
Something grated, and distracted me
Like a broken fingernail.

Trespass

I turned to you,
Smelling out warmth like a cat,
Preying on you decorously
For touch and comfort.

We always want more than we bargain for –
The particular tone of voice,
The special intimacy,
The exclusive offer.

To appear in your mind's eye
Couched in glowing terms
And under your hand in dreams
Was my desire.

But reality was more of the commonplace.
I learned to stand in line for your largesse;
To ask for nothing, and to look for less.

Underground Car Park

Worms can find their way through a maze
better after being fed chopped up worms
who have already learned how to do it.
PSYCHOLOGY TEXTBOOK

How to get out?
A minotaur would be hard put to it.

Those dim, dank walls,
Those misty pillars, bald as old trees –
Glass eyes glinting between them.

Somewhere there must be a coveted egress;
Some half-lit shaft
Or bolting-tunnel.

If only the architect were fed to me
Piece by piece,
I could absorb his plan –
Quick as sugar into the bloodstream –
And appear, to applause,
Outside on the pavement.

An Uninteresting Case

The doctor looked at my palm:
'I see a reasonable life line,' he said,
'Some travel, a dark man with a glass eye

And a lovely bungalow. Take these tablets
And drop me a line about the side-effects.
Next please.' 'Wait,' I said,

'I've come about my mother, she's depressed.'
'Who isn't?' he cried, with a basilisk look,
Chewing at his frayed stethoscope,

'But this week I'm only seeing female patients
Under forty – and next week
I retire to the seaside.'

Vauxhall

Pulling through cliffs of windows
We stop at the platform:
Murky, misty; damp haloes round the lights –
The graffiti half lost in dust.

The train gives an orgasmic shudder
And falls silent.
The few passengers gaze vacantly about.
One gives a racking sigh.

Vauxhall. The word blooms in my mind,
Opening up green vistas. Down one of them
My mother, playing the piano,
Waiting for her washing to dry, and singing tremulously:

When Lady Betty passes by
I strive to catch her bright blue eye
At Vauxhall in the morning.

Round her elbow I can just make out the words.
Her hands are crinkly from the soapsuds;
Outside, the roses catch at the blown sheets,
And in Vauxhall, it is all blossom and glances.

I smile out at the grimy wall
(*Wogs sod off – Arsenal are shit*)
And the train throbs back to life,
Sliding us on to some more ordinary place.

Vicious Circle

When I think of myself dying
My eyes fill
With sympathy for the bereaved.

Will they recover?
Will a month, a year, see them eating and sleeping again?

Well, some mourn themselves out of this world
But often the news of death seems merely – newsworthy.

The ranks close with an indelicately hasty shuffle,
It's just a meeting of old friends at the funeral
And who's going to have the silver spoons,
And off with your boots to the Oxfam shop.

It's almost enough to make you suicidal.

FROM

Moving In

(1984)

Deadlines

Sullen, they lie in their tissue paper
refusing to speak or to move their limbs.
If they know the plot, they do not like it.

The ardent hero has lost his voice:
the incestuous father has forgotten his vice
and the heroine is in her depressive phase.

What can I do? One of them labours
into a sitting position. He cranks open his mouth
and speaks. Do you come here often? he grins.

'It's the Position That Counts'

I only have to walk down the street
past the betting shop with its rainbow door strips
and the barber's window furnished with dusty Durex;

I only have to cross the road
under the railway, where the shit-littered pavements
hint at native alsatians of fearful size;

I only have to get past the bus garage –
watching out for the sudden rush of a rogue bus
at top speed, behind schedule –

and soon I come to the Common where, in a fine dusk,
I have seen rabbits scuttle at my step, and pocket themselves
like billiard balls, into the untrammelled earth.

Masters' Common Room 9 a.m.

My God, I've got the Upper Fourth first,
just when I feel like Alka Seltzer and utter hush,
and 'Yes Sir' the only spoken words,
and those whispered.

Here's the new chap – tiresomely keen
I hate him, under my smile.
I looked a bit like him
ten years ago.

Could I manage if I gave it all up,
freelanced, wrote reviews –
I've only myself to think about,
unfortunately.

Oh God, the Upper Fourth;
the late, lamented, loutish Upper Fourth.
They see in me (what I see in myself)
that I could do better.

Gardening

I've planted roseola round the door
and amenorrhoea under the window,
with a ground cover of pes planus
and spring uveitis.

Along the fence I'm training bronchiectasis
but down at the bottom it's wild
with atheroma and cystitis
and when we sit outside, the air is heady
with the blue carbuncle.

Charity

Trouble has done her good,
Trouble has stopped her trivialising everything,
Giggling too much,
Glittering after other people's husbands.

Trouble has made her think;
Taken her down a peg,
Knocked the stuffing out of her.
Trouble has toned down the vulgarity.

Under the bruises she looks more deserving:
Someone you'd be glad to throw a rope to,
Somewhere to send your old blouses,
Or those wormy little windfalls.

A Summer Afternoon

It used to take him so long
to open up: faltering footsteps,
the scrunch of chains; the tremulous key
scratching round the lock: at last a crack
for the old nose to quiver through.

That June I was busy; but in July
I knocked. Nothing stirred, only –
inside the window – great bluebottles hung,
hazed and glutted, glinting in the afternoon sun,
clotting and fringing the small panes.

A second knock dislodged a few to random motion.
Some climbed over others. There seemed to fall
a long moment of collusion:
for they did not want to come out,
and I did not want to go in.

Moving In

Well that is where the pictures hung:
Three squares; dust-rimmed and blank as a slammed door.

Were they masked, before, by Still Lives
Or scenes of Venice; or serial studies

Of an uncle coming up to bowl
In sepia white flannels; his moustache

Flaring at the batsman (off camera left)?
I forward their letters, but I do not ask.

At last it is time to mark out my territory.
I take hammer and nails; and over the squares

I superimpose my stuffed carp. Its starboard eye
Rides high, majestically, over my new room.

Coming Out

Leaning against the window,
Legs pressed languorously to the radiator,

I spot the first sign of spring
In a bleak slice of garden over the back fence.

An arm – upright as a cable-car arm –
Is trolling a duster along a washing-line,

Wiping away winter. Soon, swelling and rising
On zephyrs, the first washing is in bloom.

Loss

I

When at last she died
in the nursing home, where nuns
whispered along the Spanish-tiled passages,
she left a list, in shaky writing:

> These are my things:
> the small chair by the window,
> the picture by the bed,
> the blue ginger jar
> and the box of photographs.

I folded the paper, laid it
in the empty ginger jar
and replaced the lid.
Some things don't bear reading twice.

II

Here in this hotel room half across the world –
the air laundered; the bathroom
shiny as a new tooth –
pain floods in at last.

No one ever did all they could:
and all we did was not enough
for you. Why couldn't you go sooner –
go when the going was good?

Not too soon. Not when you were all-powerful.
A parent owes it to a child to be in keeping:
first present; then distant; and finally
absent. But all without screaming.

The Night Light on the Mantelpiece

In my dream my child was young again
and came to our room, frightened, in the night.

I lifted him on to the couch, covering him,
tucking, murmuring, love pouring down,

and awoke, crying. It is we,
who are older, who have the real fears,

wonder who we are, cling, and need
the night light on the mantelpiece.

Dorothy

After an illness in late middle age
Dorothy Wordsworth lost her reason.

They wheel me about. The daffodils
have come and gone, and William showed them to me.
They think my mind has also gone.
Sometimes I dream myself, in glory
and in freshness, back in Dove Cottage.
It is haunted by something which has not yet
happened. I see a crowd, a host of people.
They peer into all the corners of the life
which was mine and William's. I shout at them
as I wake. No one understands.
Mary strokes my hand, and William,
striding in from meadow, grove and stream,
reads me something from long ago.
He would tie up the beansticks then
while I baked loaves, my days
tied each to each by natural
love. There was such a time, but now
they wheel me about.

Bloomsbury Snapshot

Virginia's writing her diary,
Vanessa is shelling the peas,
And Carrington's there, hiding under her hair,
And squinting, and painting the trees.

Well Maynard is smiling at Duncan,
A little to Lytton's distress,
But Ralph's lying down with a terrible frown
For he'd rather be back in the mess.

There's Ottoline, planning a party –
But Leonard's impassive as stone:
He knows that they'll all sit around in deck chairs
Discussing their own and each others' affaires,
And forming, perhaps, into new sets of pairs:
And oh, how the bookshelves will groan.

A Luminary to Tea

At last you emerge up the station steps
Slice by slice; first the freckled cranium
Fringed with white; then the spectacles
Winking back the beaming afternoon, and now,
Complete and genial, you loom over me.
There was a hold-up on the District Line.

I draw you out on a modest tour:
This, then, is The Green
(*Very fine* – but your eye is impassive)
And here is the river bank, which is –
I falter – much painted. You look upstream
And then downstream. But I see
The river is running boringly today.

44

The park, also, has somehow lost its vistas
And assumed a municipal expression.

Home for tea. *No cake thank you.*
Flat as the park. I dredge up views
And old, much-trodden gossip –
But you are peering over my shoulder:
Could we watch the cricket highlights
Just for a moment? We switch hemispheres
Into a humming, electric brilliance.
A hand shoots up. A catch! The ground is
In uproar. The cat, sensing an accommodation,
Pushes its bullet head into your lap
And embarks on a long wash.

Choices

Suggested by a theme in Homecomings by C.P. Snow

The secret planner paces out our days:
    Beneath the margin of the conscious brain,
There is a thread that leads us through the maze

She saw him once, and barely met his gaze,
    And hardly knew she looked for him again.
The secret planner paces out our days.

Although he meant to go – yet still he stays;
    The pattern changes, reasons are not plain,
There is a thread that leads us through the maze.

The message in the nerves; that half-heard phrase
    That forms an incantatory refrain:
The secret planner paces out our days.

So viscerally slow, the part it plays,
Its data drawn from some unknown terrain,
The secret planner paces out our days,
There is a thread that leads us through the maze.

Self Selection

At last *Safeways*
Has made a notable contribution
To everyday philosophical thought.

SELF SELECTION is their theory, put forward
In bold caps, beside the oranges,
And who could resist it?

Who would not be pleased to carry home
A better adjusted, seamless,
Selfless self: decisive yet flexible,

Loving yet integral; cheerful
But not offensively so?
A self with poise,

Who knows a mot juste
From a put-down;
A complaint from a whine.

A brave self. A self
Who worries more about world starvation
Than his dandruff.

But what to do with the old self?
Drown it in a bucket? Leave it
Under the counter, where the boxes are?

It would follow you home.
You would feel it creeping back
Under your waistcoat.

It knows you hate change.

Accountability

The musician Bruckner was handicapped by
a counting obsession which overcame him
when he was tired.

Life is wearing me down
by a process of attrition, multiplication
and unnecessary movement –
largely on the part of birds.

The number of windows in the street
is easily achievable: furrows in a field,
berries on a branch. The thirty-seven roses
on my counterpane are unequivocal.

But the swallows make my heart race
with their terrible interweaving:
and what I dread is a clear sky
at night. Always at dusk,
I am drawn to the window. Reluctantly
I turn my face upwards.

Last Words

How he loved the bird.
Each day, between his duties with the large mammals
he would come to its cage.

The bird clung to the mesh,
powerful and black: its tool-sharp beak
working at the metal.

Little by little, the keeper's few words
lodged in its brain. One day
the feathers at its throat moved

and a gruff ventriloquist voice
spoke from its beak:
'How's the old boy then?'

The keeper didn't hear.
Last week he'd been retired, after a mauling –
Been sent off to Perth, to his one relation.

He never recovered. The bird,
fixing its listeners with a glittering eye,
uttered its question time and time again.

Tidying Up

Hear the shots at dawn.
Multiple murders are taking place
Of a sensible kind:
The culling of the deer.

Animals seen limping
May not walk again;
Animals which falter and fall
Need not apply to rise.

In principle I approve of this principle.
Such neatness and utility. Why can't we practise it?

My head itches where the metal would enter.

Survivors

Anyone could batter down the ferns
with their weak, suppliant fronds unfurling
and bending to the prevailing wind. In dry weather
fire wipes out whole acres of them.

But under your feet the new shoots are
inexorable. Bumping up, hard as beads,
they fist into hooks, into question marks,
putting on meekness all over the earth.

Postcards

The postcards flock
and settle on my doormat.

The seas are so blue
you could dip your pen in them;

villas are heavy with vines,
nothing interrupts the sun.

'All we do is eat, drink
and laze on the beach.'

But now, the spiders are trapezing
across the late asters;

travellers wander back
through airport lounges

with their miscellaneous bags,
their brown feet.

I feed the postcards
into the first fire of winter.

Blue skies darken,
villas crumble; bodies jerk

and fold. In no time
they are ash.

Perspectives

When it comes to rewriting the past
we are all into faction:

last week's faux pas can be re-choreographed,
last month's extravagance taken in to fit:

and last year's love affair totally edited –
the roles re-cast, the story line strengthened

and one's own part adapted and rendered
more rational. Darker areas of betrayal and folly

are lost, with clever lighting
and the use of perspective.

All it takes is time, rehearsal
and one's own gullibility.

Short Story

As I knocked the cup from the shelf
my mind flashed up reprises:

that glass you dropped, the dark hotel room,
my letter in the rack, your car driving away;

a masterpiece of précis.
The cup hits the floor. I turn to pick up the pieces.

Mutability

Some months after it was finished
(the raw emotions concreted over)
she saw him again, and was amazed at the change.

Surely he was shorter by at least an inch;
coarser at the neck and waist;
the endearing imperfections overtly more imperfect
and less endearing; why had he changed so much
since she stopped loving him?

She smiled in condescending sympathy:
but then, so did he.

Chance Meeting

Are we the same people –
All that love and rancour
Dried up and crumbled away?

Now we smile, ask after the children,
Pour cups of tea where once we threw them.
The antic hay has danced us all apart.

We hardly recognise old partners,
Or remember the music that sent us round
Yearning for the wrong hand.

The Innocent

'If only she would come back,' he said,
'Everything would be all right.'

What the innocent can't see
are the 'if onlys' just over the horizon,
spawning and feeding
and forming into sub-groups
of want and desire.

For a moment he thinks he's made it –
but 'Look behind you,' we cry
'Look behind you.'

Cookery

Strange how the heat both softens and hardens:
Turning sinews to gelatine
And liquid batters into crispness and substance
Or cricket-bat solidity.

Soon, I will take you and feed you
My stew. It will be thick, reddish brown,
And rich as the beginning of the world.
In it will be dark mouthfuls engorged with wine,
Crusted and melded with gold and amber tenderness.

Rumour of it will reach you from the kitchen,
Embarrassing you with saliva –
But when you eat, I shall leave the room,
For you must be alone to commune
With this dark tide, which will flood,
Like evangelism, through the blood
Under your pale accountant's skin.

Later, I will sit with you over crumbly meringues
And you will smile, under the pearls on your moustache.

Such goodness. I know it is right.
You will soften and harden for me.

Is It Anything to Worry About, Doctor?

Oh no, nothing to worry about.
We all have to go in the end. Some of us
Would envy you. Better the quick coup
Than the messy loiter. Do what you like.
Just put your affairs in order.
There's nothing much to worry about – and soon
Nothing at all.

Central Reservations

(1990)

Clay Pipes

Here is the box with the pieces of clay pipe,
stems like twigs, bowls swagged and ribbed,
all cracked and chipped; but neatly docketed
in your schoolboy hand.

They were difficult to spot on the river bank
amongst the pebbles. We spent hours
bent over like ancients, quartering the ground
(you in your first adolescence, me in my second).

The Thames mud smelled of beer from the brewery;
fishermen stood peacefully in their waders,
while we scrunched and scraped and pounced
with nervous absorption.

When two pieces jigsawed together
you gave your special, satisfied frown.

Bed

In this store window, a vast bed,
radiant white in satin, lace and crystals,
embowered, flounced and veiled: a Swan Lake –
an iced cake of a bed; unsullied, intacta.

It knows nothing of body fluids,
amorous heats, night sweats,
birthings, couplings, dyings –
such leaky businesses.

By this bed, a lover would kneel,
slender as a freesia, his samite cuff
trailing the floor. Could you relish
so immaculate a conception?

Central Reservations

I've just been taught another damn lesson.
Is there no end to them?

It's still all life tests,
crossroad decisions, multiple choices.

Even last words may be subject to assessment:
but do we have faith in the examiner?

As I ponder this, a voice issues
from clouds looming above the window:

Trust me, it booms, *we know what I am doing.*

August in the Offices

The small divorces of the summer offices
relieve the year, let in the air.

Absentees sun themselves by succulent hedgerows
or sit in rain-soaked reveries on river banks –

but their desks gather accretions; the names on their doors
have a distant, commemorative look.

Territories suffer encroachment, feuds and flirtations
lose their fine balance; but in September –

the canvas shoes flung to the back of the cupboard –
flocks of fresh memos gather for the winter.

The Claimant

There's no reasoning with gloom:
it breaks out from below the pavement
into your head, into the corners of the room.

Supposing you trace its lineage. What's the point?
Name it; it merely answers
You're the one I want.

One's Correspondence

I wrote to you to say that I'd be there
but lost the letter giving your address
and now I cannot find it anywhere.

Although I've searched until I'm in despair,
what's worrying me most is, I confess,
I wrote to you to say that I'd be there.

It came first thing on Tuesday (to be fair
the breakfast table was in quite a mess)
and now I cannot find it anywhere.

I think you said you lived in Berkeley Square
or did you say you'd moved to Inverness?
I wrote to you to say that I'd be there.

Where parties are concerned, you have a flair.
The letter said: 'Please come in fancy dress,'
and now I cannot find it anywhere.

I'm sure I wrote a note but couldn't swear
to posting it: this is an S.O.S. –
I wrote to you to say that I'd be there
and now I cannot find it anywhere.

Compassion

Waiting in the supermarket queue
with my mange-tout and steak,
I gazed abstractedly
at the shoes of the woman in front –

plastic and misshapen, sticking plaster
where one rubbed at the instep.
In her basket (her hands grey and knuckly)
some small bony meat.

She looked so illimitably patient and hopeless
that the easy tears blurred my eyes at the cash desk.
But then I went home again,
and I was so busy with my dinner party, you see.

Confession

One day, she told a stranger on a train
everything. After twenty years
she didn't find it easy to begin,
but then, encouraged by his faint, grey nods,

she fitted words together:
explanations, revelations, vindications –
the relief was enormous.
She touched her face with cambric, feeling shriven.

At the next station he rose, creakingly,
'So very nice to chat with you, but I fear
the conversation was a shade one-sided.
This wretched deafness...'

Heaven on Earth

The loveliest times in all my life
my mother told me – near the end of it –
were when I used to go to the Caledonian Market
on Tuesday mornings. I remembered her
coming home on those Tuesdays,
ruffled, animated, as from an assignation
or triumph. Once she brought back
a clockwork canary in a wire cage
which sang on two notes and gyrated
like a tiny feather duster.
When it dropped off its perch
she took it back to the stall
quivering with delicious indignation
and had it put miraculously right.
In those days, she sighed,
anything could be made better.

Diversions

In old age, confined to bed,
my mother developed a keen obsession.

Lorry jack-knifed on the M4, she would cry
as you skirted the commode to greet her:

They'll have to leave at Exit 2
and go round here – she had a map

on her bedside table:
her thin finger quivered.

Our small talk, our flowers and chocolates
washed up against a tide

of burst water mains, spillages,
contraflows. We nodded solemnly.

She'd gained a nourishing rapport
with all the road junctions in the country.

Are you sorry you never travelled?
I asked her. She shook her head

at my stupidity. Every day,
every night, she travelled.

Trouble Ahead

In the taxi, in a sweating, static
jam, you check your watch again.
Your train! You're bound to miss it.
And what about the stranger
who is meeting you? Troubled scenarios
blossom and race through your head.

Someone leans on his horn, and the hooting
spreads, like an animal cry
through a herd. A bearded man
strides back angrily from some crisis point
ahead. *Christ, can't you wait a few minutes!
Someone's dead.*

All fall silent
but it's an exasperated silence.
*Death buggers up the traffic no end.
People should die in bed.*

Choice

You're the one I boned up mah jongg for
You're the one I bought the chaise longue for
You're the one I yearn to go wrong for.

You're the one I'll garden my plot with
You're the one I'll throw in my lot with
You're the one I'll find my G spot with.

You're the one I've had my teeth capped for
You're the one my scruples were scrapped for
You're the one I get all unwrapped for:
                    You're the one.

Entrails

I am convinced that digestion is the great secret of life –
REV SYDNEY SMITH

Twenty-two feet of wonders
Twenty-two feet of woes:
Why we're obliged to have so many yards of them
Nobody really knows.

Sometimes they lie retentive,
Sometimes they're wild and free,
Sometimes they writhe and get madly expulsive
The moment you're out to tea.

Entrails don't care for travel,
Entrails don't care for stress:
Entrails are better kept folded inside you
For outside, they make a mess.

Entrails put hara-kiri
High on their list of hates:
Also they loathe being spread on the carpet
While someone haruspicates.

Twenty-two feet of wonders
Twenty-two feet of woes:
Why we're obliged to have so many yards of them
Nobody really knows.

Moscow Spring

In the Kuskova gardens
workmen lift the wooden boxes
from the delicate statues.

Tender bushes are unwrapped
from their overcoats; twigs unbend
in the melting light.

The men warm to their work;
hang their fur hats
in a row on the fence.

Faidagery

Three men in camel overcoats – coarse, moon-faced,
slicked-back hair – are sitting in the front row
of an audience.

They mutter to each other disapprovingly
then rise, button their coats
and ostentatiously leave, saying:

'I can't stand to see women committing
Faidagery.'

It's not in the dictionary: I look for it
when I wake up. But it might be in some
arcane tome or medical compendium.

One could be committing Faidagery
in all innocence.
There is always something you do
which annoys somebody.

Jessie's Bakery

*This shop, something of a cult with local inhabitants,
for its delicious hot bread, was closed by the health
authorities on the grounds that the flour was full of moths.*

Blindfold, you could find it by the reek
of stale cats. Big Jessie queens it here, her grey hair
dollied up in yellow curls, six days a week.

It takes her years to talk your loaf into a bag.
The weather never tires of hearing about itself.
Flour stirs and settles; hours lag.

In fact, time stops. Flies, as if in amber,
stiffen in syrup tarts. Sultanas scab
the shelves; the customers half remember

the world, in its complexity and pain;
and, like the lotus eaters, grow averse
to facing it again.

Frank's Journal, December 1878

That morning, it was wonderfully cold.
I put a bowl of water on the sill
and in an hour it froze. So far, so good.

The dog-cart picked me up at half-past eight,
then we collected Willie, Jack and Fred
and up we went to Earith. By the time
we started off for Welney, it was ten.

My first long run on skates. They went ahead
while I got in my stride with less despatch.
My face ached from the wind: I had to rest
by Bedford's, but I soon warmed to my work
and got to Welch's Dam by half past twelve:
the last six miles took only half an hour.

The Welney skaters – fastest in the world –
were marvellous to watch, and there were crowds
to cheer them on. The low rays of the sun
struck sparks of fiery light from skates and ice.

At the *Blue Boar* we ate a pigeon pie
and, taking biscuits and a flask of tea,
we turned for home again, against the wind.

We ran eight miles and rested by the Dam,
then down the counter wash, across the bank
and round by Hundred Foot, where just before
a lad had drowned (but no one that we knew).

We passed the Dinsdale boys on Bury Fen...
and after that I slowed, and lagged behind.
My legs were made of lead, my hands of ice;
the sun had disappeared, the sky was dark;
I prayed for strength to make myself keep on.

I can't remember how I reached my goal
but Lansdowne James was standing on the bank.

He pulled me from the ice, but I could move
no more: my skates were frozen to my feet
completely, so he took me on his back
and carried me to shelter. Such a day!
I offered prayers of thanks, and was so bold
as to petition that the ice should hold.

Wants

Like yours, my wants are simple:
security with the window ajar,

the battle without the spilt guts;
the family to throw off

and rediscover: a magical bed-post
and Life Everlasting, with my own teeth.

The Badminton Game

That morning, I awoke and went down
just as I was, in my green slippers,
to look at the hydrangea mariesii –
the only flower Clifton allows in the garden,
for he must have his trees and shrubs.

Out I crept, my slippers darkening in the dew,
and hearing a movement beside me
I turned and found Ruth. She was carrying
the racquets; and so – smiling, not speaking –
we ran between the great bushes to the net,

and there we played (quietly, of course,
so that Uncle Edward might not hear)
until the breakfast gong recalled us.
We ran up the backstairs en deshabille,
and down the front ones, decorous but tardy,

and kissed Uncle Edward; but I took care
to embrace him as he likes best, to forestall
reproof. Colour rose up behind his moustache
and his face worked silently, but then he vanished
as usual, behind *The Times*.

Albert Memorial

Passing the Albert Memorial
I remember our night of love, so-called,
which started with a concert, and went on

to the expensive hotel where we ate our supper
too much, too rich, too noisy –
the violinist, with his pander leer

fingering and bowing over the stuffed avocados
and I, like (but unlike) a Vestal Virgin
wishing I were home at my sacred hearth.

Courage! Courage! This is what is called Life.
Put down the hermit's dish and tackle
this hunk of meat – so vigorous

it nearly leaps out of its sea of sauce.
At last we are in the lift which elevates
from Gluttony to Lust. The corridors stretch

into infinity; such luxurious cells
and here by the bed is a Gideon Bible.
I open it, keen for guidance or diversion.

Too late! You bend over me,
tall as the Albert Memorial, or a tree,
take the book and tidy it away,
bored with the prologue and ready for the play.

Terribly Weak. Please Come.

Darling Mama. The hamper came today,
I never got such a jolly surprise.
But the shirts are Willie's. Mine are
one quite scarlet, and the other lilac.

*　*　*

A delightful viva voce, first in the *Odyssey*,
where we discussed epic poetry in general,
dogs and women... Of course I knew
I had got a First, so I swaggered
horribly. My poor mother is in great delight.

*　*　*

I want to be one of Her Majesty's
Inspectors of Schools. Will you
write me a testimonial?

*　*　*

My name is printed six feet high –
printed, it is true, in those
primary colours against which
I spend my life protesting, but anything
is better than virtuous obscurity.

I am perfectly happy, and hope
you will be very fond of my wife.

The baby is wonderful.
It has a superb voice,
its style is essentially Wagnerian.

We must wear cloaks with lovely linings. Otherwise
we shall be very incomplete.

*　*　*

I am much better. I go every day
and drive in a beautiful forest called
the Bois de Boulogne, and in the evening
I dine with my friend. I hope
you are taking great care of dear Mamma.

*   *   *

After the play is produced
I leave for the South of France
where I am obliged to go
for my health.

*   *   *

Bosie has insisted on stopping here
for sandwiches. He is quite like a narcissus,
so white and gold.
I hope you will enjoy my play. It is written
by a butterfly for a butterfly.

*   *   *

Dearest of all boys,
you must not make scenes with me.
They kill me. They wreck
the loveliness of life.

*   *   *

Dearest Robbie: Since I saw you, something has happened.

*   *   *

Inform the Committee of the Albemarle
that I resign my membership.

*   *   *

As I sit here in this dark cell
I blame myself.

You had no motives in life.
You had appetites merely.

*　*　*

The idea that he is wearing anything I gave him
is peculiarly repugnant to me.

*　*　*

The abscess has been running now
for the entire time of imprisonment.

*　*　*

As for my clothes, my fur coat
is all I need really. The rest
I can get abroad.

Heath was my hatter, and understands my needs.

*　*　*

My life was unworthy of an artist: now I hope
to do some work.

*　*　*

Of course I love you more than anyone else
but our lives are irreparably severed.

*　*　*

It is impossible for us to meet.

*　*　*

Everyone is furious with me
for going back to you
but they don't understand us.

*　*　*

I am sorry... but what is there in my life
for which I am not sorry?

I do think that, if we engage not to live together,
I might still be left the £3 a week.

The morgue yawns for me.
I go and look at my zinc bed there.

                    *   *   *

Friday and Saturday I had not a penny
and had to stay dinnerless in my room.

                    *   *   *

How I used to toy with that tiger, Life.

                    *   *   *

I made great friends with a young
Seminarist. He said he would not
forget me, and I do not think
he will, for every day
I kissed him, behind
the High Altar.

                    *   *   *

I have now been in bed for ten weeks.
The expenses of my illness amount
almost to £200.

                    *   *   *

TERRIBLY WEAK. PLEASE COME.

Tête-à-Tête

After supper (ratatouille, heated on his gas ring)
she remarked on a moth which circled the lamp
throwing wild shadows round the room.

When it quivered to rest on the rubber plant
they leafed through his book of lepidoptera
their knees almost touching,

they leaned over its furry, palpitating body,
their heads almost touching, and at last,
after an awkward pause,

he read aloud: *The Monarch butterfly*
knocks the female to the ground
and copulates with her wherever she falls.

Almost at once, she looked at her watch and,
murmuring politely, slipped from the door
and flew down the steps to the street.

Bargaining

He wakes to his old obsession.
Nothing has changed.

He will trawl the streets
as usual, for a chance meeting;

he will plead, as usual
with her answering machine.

But in a flash revelation
he knows what is needed:

a sacrifice. Unknown powers
must be placated.

He polishes his car,
drives to the waste ground

behind the Odeon. There
he sets fire to it.

His second love is immolated
to gain his first.

Necessary sadness; a cleansing
blaze. Ash settles

in his thinning hair.
The tears are a relief.

He turns towards her house. His ear
anticipates the joyous peal

of her doorbell:
her cry of surrender.

Chacun

'That weekend, she lay on the bed
as usual, smooth and distant in my arms.
We seemed set for our normal parts –
I, noisy, active, verging on the hysterical;
she marmoreal, abstracted
among the rucked and musky sheets.

And then, this day, she moved:
her body moved to me.
Her teeth clenched, a tremor broke in her
like power through a fault in the earth.

I swung over, hot as fur, and fought her
to conclusion. We did not speak.
If I laughed, it was only briefly:
but when I left, she slammed the door on me,
lock, hook and bolt.'

Leaving Jenkins

(extracts from the diary of a young schoolmaster in 1876)

Sunday

As I had no timepiece, my own
being at the menders, I got up late.

A typical Sunday: the Iron Church in the morning,
Sunday School this afternoon (the boys unruly

both in Jenkins' class and in my own);
a capital sermon this evening.

Tuesday

Tomorrow I shall have been on this earth
for 21 years. I have resolved, with God's help,

to give a better account of myself within the next year,
if spared. Walked to Finsbury Park with Jenkins.

Tonight I am reading Pepys' Diary. He seems a man
utterly devoid of real, sound principles.

Wednesday

Received three letters on my birthday,
from my mother, my father and Fred.

Took singing in the Senior Room
while Mr Timpson examined my class in dictation.

Jenkins is suffering from indigestion. Went with him
to Dr Hill, who charged him 1/6d. and told him nothing.

Saturday

Went to look at the Great Eastern terminus.
It is very tastily got up.

This evening, Mr Sherlock from upstairs
brought down his galvanic battery,

vacuum tubes, microscope and organ accordion.
Talked until 2 a.m. Other lodgers displeased.

Saturday

To Beavis to be measured for a suit
of summer clothes (55/-). Jenkins ordered a waistcoat.

At last made up my mind to see Henry Irving
in *The Bells*. Felt better for it –

if all theatres were carried on like this,
there would be little harm done.

Sunday

The sermon this morning dealt with
vicarious sacrifice: discussed with Jenkins.

Tonight, the Rev. Marmaduke Millar told us
why he believed in angels; it was quite scientific.

So tired, I rode home in a public vehicle
though I cannot think it right on a Sunday.

Saturday

To the City to see the progress
of the Metropolitan Railway.

My face was much swollen from the wind
and the druggist gave me camomile flowers,

poppy heads and a black draught.
Jenkins came round this evening and read to me.

Thursday

I am accepting the post at Woodhurst School
at £80 plus £5 as Clerk of the Board.

Jenkins is sorry that I am going.
I believe I have done him good:

I have tried to instil in him
a taste for literature, and he has taken

to the Popular Educator; but he wonders
what he will do when I have gone.

History

Some changes come so slowly:
nothing happens, yet something is happening

The boy is on a slow dissolve into youth.

The creeper covers the pergola
though you sat under it for days
and not a leaf moved.

Her heart cools to you perhaps
but when did this begin –

was it that day when her gaze
strayed to someone for a moment;

or when she first moved her hand
away, like this?

If You Come

The birds come to feed me. Yesterday
one brought bread and today I have a nut, a snail
and a berry, red as your mouth.

Moving air sighs in the eaves:
La belle indifférence I hear, as nightfall
robs the trees of a dimension.

Messages, of course, I disseminate freely:
one behind the clock, one in the knife drawer,
one into my letterbox – an oubliette in its own right.

If you come, take the aerial route,
alighting near the embankment
where the backless cupboards and bony umbrellas

are all pierced through with heartsease and dock,
branches strive through the brickwork
and the paving is grouted with moss.

In the Summerhouse

In the summerhouse
you cannot hear your children crying.

Plaintive sounds fan out
from the far windows

and dissipate into the canopy of trees.
Everything loosens in the heat,

petals, buds, muslin.
Hands unpin your hair...

now you hear nothing,
but the tick of a watch.

The Last Great Fog

The fog came down at four,
thick and impassive at the windows,
and suddenly the office was an island.

You walked me home through this strangeness.
The buses had given up. An occasional car
faltered along the road, its lights describing
swirling cylinders of nothingness.

The fog set us free. We laughed at everything.
We were abroad, unattached, in lunatic spirits:
we clung, falling about on kerbstones.
You pulled me inside your overcoat
and the tweed tasted of fog.

The next day dawned bathetically fine.
You worked without remission at your desk
and I at mine.

Waking in the Garden

I think I know where I am.
A rumbling train shivers the ants in the grass,
a branch shifts and groans,
my cheek is creased
by a rug of folded hills.

I cannot make my eyes open.

Someone may be near me.
A voice cries 'havoc' –
but who would use such a word?
My heart knocks – the only part of me
which can move.

A doll I had once
would not open her eyes;
her blind lids were shellac pink
and blank as insolence.
We punished and punished her.

In the silver distance
glasses ring with laughter.
Music spools out of a window
and is pulled back in again.
I concentrate my will –

prise open a crack of light
which falls on the yolk of a daisy,
on the mountainous pores of my arm,
on a gargantuan hand
which flexes itself in the grass.

Lost Belongings

The preamble was brilliantly put together:
the downland path leading to the horizon
under fresh snow; a spaniel running back to us
with a stick. We bend towards him, and as we walk on
you take my hand in yours. A close-up shows
my shocked delight. But the face
is strangely unlike my own.

We are seen growing closer. The theatre seats
at your own play; my friends becoming envious;
the first kiss, in that shadowy room
with the blue chairs. We seem set
for a life of bliss and press coverage

until I awake from this grotesque miscasting,
cooling down from euphoria to my real self.

It must have been someone else's dream
drifting in the ether, attaching itself
to the wrong night's sleep – like a video
from the wrong box, viewed by mistake
but with serendipitous delight.

Modus Vivendi

Each night, as he played patience
she stood behind his shoulder.

'Jack on Queen,' she would cry
just before he spotted it himself.

How was it, then, that she murdered him
rather than the reverse?

Some games have rules
which are the very devil to understand.

Visiting Time

In the ward, after the stroke,
he could not remember whom he liked
and whom he disliked.

A young man with reddened eyes
held his hand. He could not name him
though the tie seemed familiar.

When a woman swept in with flowers
and seemed to assume intimacy
he feigned sleep.

The Slipping Glimpse

I am into the business
of uninvention.

My desk is loaded with applications:
I am quite private behind my in-tray.

The procedures, you can imagine
are tortuous: the paperwork, the manual work,

the research, the lasering out of information
from human brain cells.

Often there are misunderstandings
about my scope and capability:

(Famine? Disease?
I do not set myself up against God.)

My prime achievements would mean nothing to you
success conceals success.

You may hear a phrase, perhaps,
cut off from its context –

muffled sounds on the radio of a passing car;
words heard through a door as it closes.

Hour by Hour

The number of hours in stock for each of us
is tiresomely finite. Stamped
and docketed, they grin up at you
from the shelves of the cellar
where it is too dark to count.

How to use the ones at the front
is the first problem: frighteningly they melt away –
in bus queues, in adversarial dramas over drains;
in sleeping things off. Sometimes someone
scoops up their whole shelf-full and throws them
out of the window, murmuring
'It's the only language they understand.'

Your Laugh

Your laugh, wide and benign enough
to swallow the world.

No one laughing like that
can protect themselves against attack.

The sofa shakes its sides in sympathy.
Smiles bud out round the room.

Your arching, glinting, risky laugh.

Dear Mother

I can't put my finger on it
but he's acting silent
and typing out lists of grievances.

On the boat he stood me near the rail
and told me: *lean over,*
look down at the fish.

Now he's booking our vacation.
The brochure shows cliff paths, deep seas,
lonely islands.

Don't worry he sometimes says
if Fate should come between us.
We can meet again on the other side.

'It's Up to You'

'When he's in a rage – teeth glinting
through the beard (which I want to touch),
eyes as hot as boiled marbles,
it's like walking on the edge of murder:
I know that game.

Once, when I was three
my mother left me in the kitchen,
a sharp knife on the table.
Be a good girl. Don't touch the knife.

I wrapped my finger in my skirt
and watched the red soak through.
I liked it. You don't have to cry.
It's up to you.'

Mutual Assured Destruction

Once they would eat from the same plate
fat black cherries, millefeuilles,
mouthfuls of fragrant melon.

It was always Tea for Two in those days,
but slowly the taste turned bitter;
the songs slurred into silence.

Now, he sleeps in the basement
and her bed is locked upstairs, the sheets
stiff, right-angled, unyielding.

The solicitors have the matter in hand.
Thick white envelopes
tongue through the letterbox.

At post time, they hover in the hall
at the edges of neutral territory,
awaiting despatches.

The Letter

I read your letter: then I took a knife
and went into the garden. There was much
that needed doing: everything in leaf
and flower, grossly intertwined; each branch

a mess of sappy green. I pruned the vine
until the twitching stalks lay in a pile.
I pulled the red camellia blossoms down
and ground them into fragments with my heel.

The fruit trees next; and how the ladder shook
with my good work. The limbs were hard to burn –
the buds curled up and shrivelled in the shock.

The willow's vulgar, semaphoring green
was last. The stump shone pale above the earth,
neat as a tooth set in a hungry mouth.

Love Song

The focus widens from the inward eye,
The convalescent half forgets his pain:
What matters is the weather in the sky
And I have fallen out of love again.

The prisoner has slipped beneath the wire;
The hawk kicks out for freedom, from the glove,
The will shakes off its burden of desire,
And I, thank God, have fallen out of love.

Two Pheasants

That first evening
they had left the suburbs behind them
and were driving through flat fields
under the vast Suffolk sky;
and as he took her hand,
after changing from third to fourth
out of a bend, he said
Will you come to me tonight?
and in the field she saw two pheasants,
split-second brilliant in the low sun,
and he added: *Look, there are two pheasants*
and she said: *Yes, yes, yes.*

The Sack

One Monday, when I rushed out late for work,
an empty, pale-grey plastic sack was huddled
by the gate. Should I take it round to the dustbin?
Later, perhaps.

When I got home, it had wandered down the road,
wrapped itself round a lamp post and was flapping.
It caught my eye. Of course, a sack
cannot wave.

Somehow I got used to seeing it about.
Thursday was dustbin day, but on Friday
it appeared again – breaking cover, perhaps,
from behind a hedge.

It had certain childlike traits:
dragging at one's legs for attention;
failing to pursue a fixed course of action; inspiring
a wry affection.

Sometimes at dusk – for a joke –
it took on fanciful, chimerical forms
and lurked, changing its shape,
behind the postbox.

It was a pantomime of versatility. Some days
it slapped up and down on the pavement.
Once it undulated up a tree. It hated the wet
more than anything.

Disconcertingly, this morning it has gone.
No one has seen it. It is not in anyone's front garden,
and I do not like to knock and ask
if it is round the back.

Things come and go, and when they go,
you feel the lack.

Waiting

The best place, when he is fractious,
is the British Museum, Egyptian Room.

There she sits on a bench
waiting for him, waiting for the time to pass.

She has waited for him in surgeries,
in special schools, in workshops;

waited for signs of improvement:
for the tide to turn.

Now he is peering at the embalmed animals
close-bandaged in their leak-marked linen.

He knocks on the glass with his knuckle
at the skinny cat sitting up tall,

the baby bull, the ducks and,
next to the crocodile, his own face

matching grin for grin. He raps harder
and she takes his arm.

Leave them alone. They won't wake up.
Hand in hand they walk away down the stairs

out past the pillars. She winds his scarf
tightly round him against the cold.

Degree Ceremony

Other mothers shed a discreet tear
but I found it impersonal:
so much Latin, so much fancy footwork,

so many students in ritual subfusc –
and you, of course,
the only really interesting one.

Later, in the car park, we kissed goodbye,
I to drive back to London,
you to stay with friends.

But I can never get out of Oxford
and finally, turning a corner,
I found you once more, walking towards me.

The laughter was helpless and difficult to stop.
How often can you say goodbye?
I thought of Alice, falling into a pool
of her own tears, and getting lost in it.

A Friendship

He made restless forays
into the edge of our marriage.
One Christmas Eve he came late,
his dark hair crackling with frost,
and ate his carnation buttonhole
to amuse the baby.

When I had a second child
he came to the foot of my bed at dusk
bringing pineapples and champagne,
whispering 'Are you awake?' –
singing a snatch of opera.
The Nurse tapped him on the shoulder.

At the end, we took turns at his bedside.
I curled up in the chair; listened to each breath
postponing itself indefinitely.
He opened his eyes once and I leaned forward:
'Is there anything you want?'
'Now she asks,' he murmured.

Choosing To Be a Swan

(1994)

Choosing To Be a Swan...

was not one of my best moves –
the balancing so tricky, the flapping
so draughty, the little loosened
feathers getting up her nose so that

she sneezed and shuddered
when stillness could have been helpful
and lay exhausted when shuddering
would have been acceptable.

When she laid the egg, her husband
was all rolling eyes and ironical looks,
but sensibly kept his mouth shut.
I twisted thunderbolts between my fingers,

but let him live on. The egg
will hatch forth a boy and a beautiful
peaceful daughter called Helen.
What more could a cuckold ask for?

Cars

Beside the railway lines
cars are waiting – metal pets
parked in abutting flocks
cooled by absence: witnesses
to strife, aggrandisement, love
adultery, death.

They die too. In car graveyards
they lie jumbled, piled
like animals awkwardly mating,
waiting to be transmuted,
crushed to metallic essence,
finally overtaken.

Wheel Fever

May 1877

Frank Reynolds has ordered a *Coventry*,
48 inches high and with all
the new improvements.

But it cost £14, and I am afraid
to sink so much money – it would be almost
three months of my salary.

All the fellows in the village
have bicycle fever, and none
more than myself.

* * *

Rode on Aubrey's wooden cycle
into Warboys, to see a Spider-Wheel
which Monty has for sale.

But the tyres were tied on
with pieces of twine, so I did not
part with my cash.

* * *

I've done it! I could not bear to wait
any longer. I now possess a *Coventry*
(without the new improvements).

Before I paid, I took it for a spin
but lost the treadle,
landed in a heap

and had to have it taken back
in the cart, and put together.
But after that

I rode off round the lanes
as right as twelve o'clock.
and pleased as Punch.

* * *

Coming back from a spin today, I met
Mr Dodds with his cartload of bread.
He must have known

that horses shy at bicycles, but
he did not get down, and sure enough
his wretched animal

reared, backed into the dyke, and emptied
22 stone of bread and 6 stone of flour
into the water.

* * *

Set out with James Black, to ride
to the prayer meeting, but
by Redman's corner

he ran into me, knocked me off,
broke my handle, bent my treadle, and fell
on top of me.

* * *

I am receiving unpleasant letters from
Mr Dodds. I do not believe that flour
can be so dear.

Unlike Aubrey or Frank Reynolds,
I can now ride my bicycle
with arms folded.

* * *

I was riding my bicycle with my arms
folded on my way to Doddington,
when I hit a stone

and pitched on my head. Managed to get up
and stagger on, covered with blood
and feeling faint.

Of course I could not help Uncle
in the shop. The carrier put his pony in
and took me home.

* * *

Could not move this morning, so stiff
and sore. My bicycle will take three days
to put right.

I miss it dreadfully. Frank Reynolds
does not seem keen on the idea
of lending me his.

But I have had a carrot poultice put on
my eye and I shall soon be fit enough
to ride again.

Surprised on a Train

Five strangers are sleeping here:
so close, I could touch them
so close, they could touch me.

By the time I caught the train
they were neatly stacked above
muffled and inert in the darkness.

Shelved, we hurtle forward
hour after hour. Which
is the stentorian breather?

At last, the first light draws
a rectangle round the door.
A foot dangles down beside me:

it is large, blunt, tanned.
On the instant, I extrapolate
burliness, machismo, chest curls;

but it is followed down
by a small, dishevelled lady
with a faded floral sponge-bag.

The Covetous Cat

Because the common is remote
they walk along hand in hand.

On the path ahead of them
some bird-lover has scattered bread

and in the middle of it a plump cat crouches
chewing at the crusts.

Cats don't really like bread, the man remarks
he only wants it because it's someone else's.

Like you, she thinks,
withdrawing her hand slightly.

Jump

They were given the bedroom
with the three dolls' houses.

She thought that he, being an analyst,
would involve her in symbolic play,

moving the doll figures about:
Why have you put the child in the attic?

*Why is the mother doll lying
under the table?* – that sort of thing.

Not at all. He simply kicked off his shoes,
flopped on his bed and went to sleep.

She pulled out the doll from under the table
and put her on the windowsill.

Jump! she whispered, *It's your big chance.*

Politeness

They walked awkwardly along the towpath
bumping together, because his arm
was round her shoulder. He was saying:
I shall always remember this walk.
I'll never forget last night.
I'll never forget you. Oh God.

After a pause, she made a short
non-committal noise. The morning had turned
wet and dark. She felt dilapidated by the rain
and of course had forgotten her umbrella
due to the unexpected turn of events.
Trust me, he said, *you will, won't you?*

Trust him to what, she wondered.
Which men could one trust? Any man
carrying a musical instrument, perhaps?
Any man walking along reading a book?
Most doctors – with reservations about those
wearing bow ties. *Trust you to what?* she asked.

To never let you down, he said,
splitting the infinitive, crushing her
against his wet tweeds. She fought
for breath as he loomed over her.
Little one, I can't let you go.
I'll be back on Thursday. Expect me.

So many imperatives. The situation
had become unwieldy. She longed
for buttered toast, looked furtively
at her watch. *I know, I know, we have*
so little time. The suffocating squeeze
into the spongy lapels.

I've never felt like this before.
Have you ever felt like this before?
Fatigue and embarrassment were
all too familiar to her. She stirred the leaves
with the toe of her boot. *No,* she said
politely. *Not exactly like this.*

In the Conservatory

Though we spring apart,
my earring, caught in your beard,
winks indiscreetly.

Prey

Outside, in the cherry tree
a wood pigeon is trampolining –
grey wings outspread – trying to catch
the shiny fruit.

On the windowsill the black cat
quivers and bristles. His covetous eye
is green as glass, his teeth ache to crunch
feather and bone.

The tiny drama takes you to the window.
Don't move. I'm just getting the feel
of the shading at your throat: the siren curve
of your mouth.

Egged on by Passion –

he attired himself in terylene,
scraped his fingernails
with the grapefruit knife, plucked
the strings of his hair across
his scalp and realigned them
at the mirror until it was so late
that he had to run to confront her.

As usual, she was preoccupied –
locking up the library
and fishing in her bag for some
lost object, so failed
to notice him, or to hear
his tentative murmur, or
the faint drumming of his head
on the municipal wall behind her.

Angela on My Mind

Outside my window pane, the sky is blue.
I know I should get up and start the day –
I cannot move, I'm thinking about you.

I phone my office, say I have the flu:
they claim they haven't noticed I'm away.
Outside my window pane, the sky is blue.

Why did you leave me for that awful Hugh?
as I recall, you told me he was gay.
I cannot move, I'm thinking about you.

I dare say it was just you'd had a few
and he mistook you for an easy lay.
Outside my window pane, the sky is blue.

But why did you respond? I wish I knew.
The note you left was curt, and didn't say.
I cannot move, I'm thinking about you.

Am I awake? Is all this really true?
Then who's beside me under my duvet?
Outside my window pane the sky is blue.
I cannot move, I'm thinking about you.

Shopper

I am spending my way out
of a recession. The road chokes
on delivery vans.

I used to be Just Looking Round,
I used to be How Much, and
Have You Got it in Beige.

Now I devour whole stores –
high speed spin; giant size; chunky gold;
de luxe springing. Things.

I drag them round me into a stockade.
It is dark inside; but my credit cards
are incandescent.

Soothsayer

I'm sure you will be very happy with this bra, Madam,
she said, her manicure seriously red as she tapped the till.
Of course I did not ask her how she knew.

Who is rude enough to challenge the clairvoyant,
the diagnostician, the prognosticator?
But she was right. As soon as she folded up

the lacy garment – its ticket swinging insouciantly –
and handed it across the counter
in its raspberry-pink bag, my spirits rose.

Outside, traffic parted for me like the Red Sea:
the sun appeared and gilded passers-by
who nervously returned my random smiles.

The days, the weeks, wore on in a numinous haze
of goodwill. Who knows why? Be cynical if you must:
I only record the sequence of events.

Adaptability

It sprang to life
in the airing cupboard –

shouldering the clothes aside
with its virile thrusting –

and soon burst out of the closet
into four coral ear trumpets.

Suburban insects stared in briefly
through the windows, fearing

for their sanity. Such power!
Even the stamens arched forward like gestures.

Now, the amaryllis is tendered
like ordinary tokens of civility –

the chocolates, the crimped carnations:
How nice – an amaryllis.

We are too adaptable. We grow used
to the unthinkable event.

The Idea

Standing idly at the window, she decides
to introduce her two friends, A and B
to each other. They are sure to get on.

At first they do not;
and then they do – warming
to badinage over the ratatouille.

Weeks later, someone remarks:
A and B are on holiday together.
A postcard arrives, signed by both,

funny and silly, with a view of a lake.
She stands at the window, chipping away
at the flaking paint for something to do.

Single Parent

Because she shares the bedroom with the baby
she undresses in the dark
and tonight her underclothes flash

and crackle in the dry air, like
miniature lightning, like
silver fireworks. It reminds her

of strobe lights, and her old crowd.
She trips and cracks her head on the bedstead
but of course must not cry out.

Our Life in Cars

Long before our first mortgage
we racketed round in that old Rolls Royce –
fifty pounds' worth of worm-holed woodwork
balding tyres and eccentricity, bought in a pub
from an itinerant Irishman.

Winding the glass partition up and down
between us was our first game; perching
on three feather pillows, I was high enough to drive.
One winter an old lady slept in it for a week
in the road outside.

But we had to part with this students' rag
of a car, grow into something safer and wiser,
with a petrol gauge and locks. The years passed soberly,
until I rode some late night taxis, and you broke out
into your Jag.

Immortality

Unwittingly, I have discovered
the secret of immortality.

But already my life is in hazard
from lobbyists and special interest groups;

stone masons, actuaries, younger sons,
environmentalists. Naturally

I have become reclusive. The grass outside
has forgotten the feel of a foot.

From the window I watch the dissolution
of my barns; the encroachment of shrubs.

Once there were paths, but now
the spotted laurels have closed their ranks:

they grow towards me, sombre as undertakers.

Blackheath
September 9th 1876

I never was in such a crush
in all my life: and just at two,
the rain came down in torrents.

The steam from our clothes
formed a heavy mist above our heads.
And still they came, thousands upon thousands.

107

At last the barriers gave way.
Many lost their footing in the rush
while I was carried forward by the crowd
and ended up before the speaker's stage.

When the great man arrived
there was a huge ovation.
All who had hats and lungs
employed them with a will.

He looked like one
who'd done his work about the world:
deep furrows on his face,
a few grey locks on his neck,
yet still a flashing eye.
Mrs Gladstone stayed a step behind.

For more than an hour he spoke
and from the crowd, hardly a murmur.
We drank in his words.

Russia, he said, had been our enemy
but now that she had changed her tune,
she was our friend.

At last he left us, to tremendous cheers.

The rain, which had ceased when he began,
now began as he ceased.

What a day it had been!
In our heavy, sodden clothes,
we moved away like sleepwalkers
waking to our ordinary lives.

Just Until

So I said to the Casting Director
I've got until April 10th
and she said to me

I think there's some mistake.
It's a grey-haired man we need all right
but it's only one line of dialogue.

One line! And I'd trolled right up
to Dean Street on the sodding tube.
One line! What would my agent say?

When I worked with Dickie that time
he used to tell me: It's all yours now lovey.
The sky's the limit.

Well yes. In the end I thought
I might as well. Just for a lark.
Just until something turns up.

Thin Ice

What I'm trying to do
is to get right through to the end
without anyone noticing
(or saying to my face)
that I am an immature person who is
only pretending to be an adult.

Thresholds

Sometimes the temptation
to step over the last heartbeat
into a different world
is hard to resist.

Held in the headlights
of some profound despair
he sits tight, hangs on,
smiles when spoken to.

But round his feet he sees
cracks opening
and from their depths,
something tentacular is uncoiling.

Choir Practice

Feeling bold, she permits herself
a furtive glance into his open mouth
as she faces him, singing her heart out.

Her hymn sheet fibrillates,
agitating waves of eau de Cologne.
Her neck tenses with longing.

Once, he hung his coat over hers
on a peg in the vestry, and afterwards
her jacket smelled deliciously

of brandy and tobacco, and on its
velvet collar lay a silver hair:
portent, memento, treasured keepsake.

Mr and Mrs R and the Christmas Card List

Shall I cross them off?
It's twenty years since we last met.

Of course Mr R and I once thought
we were made for each other –

Ah, that heart-stopping moment
by the kitchen sink, when he took off

his spectacles and fiercely kissed me.
But all that lasted less than a week

and what I recall more vividly
is Mrs R's good advice:

*Always plunge your lemons in hot water
before you squeeze them.*

One more year perhaps.

Hoi!

If you are fond of love-making, try
not to be a camel in your next incarnation
for their libido depends

on massive ingestion of a small
yellow flower, which is often struck
by drought, thus posing the camel

and his cameleer many problems,
both erotic and financial. Also, camels
(if we believe the experts)

might have become extinct without humans
to assist them in their sexual congress,
lugging and positioning their awkward bodies –

which otherwise tend to overbalance –
and holding them in position during
mating with encouraging slaps

and cries of *hoi*. What is more,
foreplay in the camel
consists of foaming at the mouth.

Incubus

Yesterday
a trouble moved in on you.
and now, this morning,
it crouches on the bedpost
plain as a gargoyle.
Try to enjoy your breakfast.
Try not to notice
its claws in your neck.

Mrs Scipio's Umbrella

Buttoning himself into a clean shirt
at his bedroom window, he saw old Mrs Scipio
next door having tea in her garden
under a striped umbrella
evidently about to eat
a very elaborate piece of cake.

When he drew back his curtains in the morning,
Mrs Scipio was still there,
her head fallen sideways, the cake
half eaten, the striped umbrella
ballooning in the wind, like a sail
anxious to take off across water.

The Night He Had Thirty-Two Pints

I meant to put your roses in a jug
but right at the beginning of the shift
they brought this boy in. It was touch and go.
Another stabbing – much like all the rest.
The hangers-on were getting in the way,
drinking from cans and shouting their complaints.
Someone must have sent for the police
but we were busy pouring in the blood –
pint after pint – and most of it ran out
on swabs and landed wetly in the bin
together with his T-shirt – dyed maroon
and scissored up through LAY ONE ON FOR ME.
He had two pints for each year of his life.
The clerk rang up his mother and she came
half wild – we heard her shouting at the desk.

Later, I saw her sitting on a bench
subdued and shaking, chattering her teeth
against a mug of tea. Her eldest son
lay like a bone, a conduit, a test
of what we could achieve. At half past three
we sent him up to Wilkins in T 5.

Despite the rush, the night dragged on for years.

We didn't win...
                    sorry about the flowers.

The Optimist

My father, in his last hospital bed
on the eve of a critical operation,
negotiated to buy from another patient
an electric razor, slightly faulty.
My mother, realist to the end
discouraged this purchase.

They argued the pros and cons
until the porter came with the trolley.
It was something to talk about
at that time, which is so awkward –
awkward and sad as waiting for a lover
to be carried away, waving, in a train.

Harriet

The cat drowses in an ambush of flowers;
each tree sits in its dish of shadow
against the faultless blue.

The world and his wife
are lazing away the hours, in retreat
until the resurrection of teatime.

Two days old, you lie
provisionally silent, waiting for night to cue
your rich, nocturnal, operatic life.

Pastoral

He pushes the pram, straight-armed,
away from the scrap yard, over the lumpy field
towards the further edge, where the M 25
bites into the boundary. His grandson
bounces, stoical and woolly-hatted.

He tries to map out the place
where he picnicked fifty years ago
with Hazel Jones. Fish paste sandwiches
and Tizer, warm from dusty saddlebags.
She stung her leg and he spat on it for her.

He imagines her rising in front of him
out of a mist, her brown hair swinging –
like a shampoo commercial. But God grant
he never meets her in the flesh – to compare
their hip joints, their grandchildren's teeth.

Sunday Lunchtime

The whirlpools of the launderette
do not recognise the Sabbath,

so the air in Worple Street
smells of soapsuds and roast beef.

The Church of Healing is silent
with endeavour – and the Oddfellows

have gathered in their Hall –
now they'll be there till evening.

Mr Patel leans on his counter
and reads about HEAVEN ON EARTH –

A celestial city discovered by *Sunday Sport*
as a change from sex. In the street

Concorde glides across car windows,
noisy as hell, but tiny as a paper dart.

The Star and the Birds

In the New Year, it starts with
a star. They point to it on her X-ray –
white, fragile, filamented,
sinister as a footstep in a dark alley.

She packs a bag, reads her horoscope.
On the ward the trolleys come and go
freighted with figures,
white-capped, whey-faced, dopey.

Taking his coarse pen (*Excuse me*)
the houseman draws an arrow
on her breast. It points to her heart
like some ironic early Valentine.

The ceiling of the anaesthetic room
is painted – its theme is zoological.
She watches the tropical birds
blur in a mêlée of bright wings.

At home her kitchen,
under its fine frost of dust,
listens to the answering machine
whirring and parroting.

Here Today

Whether to get the cheaper
or the more expensive stair-carpet

is the problem. The salesman asks me:
Are you the only person living in your house?

What next? Must I offer up my age,
state of health, genetic profile?

I point to the cheaper, shorter-life carpet.
Annoyingly he nods in agreement.

Tabula Rasa

At eighty, he set himself the task
of repainting his rooms. He worked slowly,
wheezing up and down the folding steps.

He chose the blue of his old cricket club tie;
the half-recollected gold of his wife's hair
when they first met in Rawalpindi;

and an ash-grey, which brought to mind
his son's death – that dark year
of hope and despair

In the evenings he was meticulous
with his white spirit, laying out the brushes,
battening down the lids of the tins.

Nine days after finishing, he keeled forward
over *The Times*, and closed his eyes
on a final view of his hearthrug.

Young couples came to view the property:
Perfect. We'll only need to give the place
a couple of coats of brilliant white.

Last Haiku

No, wait a minute,
I can't be old already:
I'm just about to

The Back
and the Front of It

(2000)

Apologia

My life is too dull and too careful –
even I can see that:
the orderly bedside table,
the spoilt cat.

Surely I should have been bolder.
What could biographers say?
She got up, ate toast and went shopping
day after day?

Whisky and gin are alarming,
Ecstasy makes you drop dead.
Toy boys make inroads on cash
and your half of the bed.

Emily Dickinson, help me.
Stevie, look up from your Aunt.
Some people can stand excitement,
some people can't.

The Back and the Front of It

While she marvels at the brilliance
of the peacock, he walks off to study
its back, the dun-coloured feathers,
the muscular plaque which raises the fabulous fan,
the picking-through-broken-glass gait.

While she relishes linen and silver,
leather-bound menus, rosy light
gleaming on brilliantined waiters
he tries to catch a glimpse
of the steamy, sweating kitchens.

And while she is smitten by the tightrope walkers,
their sequins flashing perilously from side to side;
the peachy acrobats with their hoops of fire
and the haughty Balinski Brothers, golden limbed
in their human pyramid –

he escapes to the rear of the tent
and joins the jugglers as they knock back
bottles of stout, pick at loose bits
of shine and glitter, belch, yawn,
rub their ankles, pick their teeth.

These two are always out of step.
Surely it can't last, but which
will be the first to stray? This is the question
which brings the clowns running,
with their jibes, their pointing fingers.

Taking a Taxi to a Wedding

My driver is on his second marriage:
'It's a gamble isn't it?' he says.
The first one was a long disappointment
but now he's happy – delirious almost.
They holiday in France: red wine
and camping come into the story
repeatedly. The new wife loves both.
She also makes tea for his cricket team.
I imagine her blonde hair swinging
over the bread and butter, her short skirt
riding up over tanned thighs. But
'She's older than me,' he adds,
slipping, eel-like, through an amber light,
'and she's mad about me.' He elaborates;
touches in frank details of their love...
All this between Putney and Ladbroke Grove.

Rewards

To those who have
shall be given:

the prize to the winners
lovers to the beautiful,

tributes to the rich,
empires to the bold.

Settle the meek
into their corners

for an interminable wait.

The Go-Between

My fiancé, bitchy to the last,
gave me as a parting gift a parrot
whose only tongue was Greek. But by the way
it spoke, I felt quite sure the bird
insulted me. His spiteful eye shot messages
of hate, and at the end of every speech
he climaxed on a fusillade of shrieks.

I bought a textbook on demotic Greek;
I joined a class; struck up a loose rapport
with waiters in a local Greek café
(a grave mistake – but that's another tale)
still nobody could give a clear account
of what the bird's discourse could mean.

                                              At length
I taught him certain Anglo-Saxon words
and sent him back by cab. He disappeared
shouting the worst obscenities I knew,
turning the air a rich and vibrant blue.

'The Unexamined Life is not Worth Living'

Taking the hint from Socrates,
he examined his life daily –
that unwieldy, shape-shifting thing.
Under a microscope, bits of it
looked promising, bits of it moribund.

His preoccupations remained constant:
first, how to become magnetic and rich
without getting out of bed too early
in the morning; next, how to stay calm
in the face of incipient baldness.

Natural Selection

Get rid of that Dog
he frowned – but died himself. She
and Dog exchanged smiles.

Cut

I don't like the company you're keeping:
fringe musicians, boom operators,
best boys. Why can't you be like your father
and polish up a decent game of golf?
That's where he found me, you know,
at the nineteenth hole.

Things to do?
But you've only just come.

Twelve Things I Don't Want to Hear

Assemble this in eight straightforward steps.
Start with a fish stock, made the day before.
The driver has arrived but, sadly, drunk.
We'll need some disinfectant for the floor.

Ensure all surfaces are clean and dry.
There's been a problem, Madam, I'm afraid!
We'd better have the manhole cover up.
Apologies, the doctor's been delayed.

I'd love to bring a friend, he's so depressed.
They've put you on the camp bed in the hall.
There's just one table left, perhaps you'd share?
I know it's midnight, but I had to call…

Birth Day

The ear will know first – that complexity
of cochlea, stirrup, drum.

But the phone is silent.

Somewhere, on rucked sheets,
you are pushing, thrashing, groaning
in a rush of sweat and blood.

Here, we gaze absently from the window

at the ice-cream-white buds of the magnolia
splitting out of their brown jackets. Time stops.

It has given up trying to match the clock.

Get a Life

When the child was born
there were long faces and tears
but after a while, despair was folded away
and planning began.

The baby's feet
flexed and grasped, practised
their stand-in role.
The baby smiled on cue, generously.

Later, she rolled, bounced,
sang, drew a house with her feet
and put herself in the garden.
She gave herself arms

and ordinary hands. Stopped.
Rubbed them out
using her special long rubber
and sat silent till tea time.

Onward and upward: a stony path,
a sunny nature, a profession.
People bring their troubles to her desk.
Her light burns on into the night.

Insomnia

It's like waiting for someone to leave –
someone tedious, garrulous
and worryingly manic.
Someone full of reminiscences
which you don't want to hear about.

It's like waiting for something
to be taken away – something
with a buzz as maddening as tinnitus;
something you've grown tired of, which is
taking up space.

These things multiply, creak and throw shadows
round the room. They start asking
upsetting questions.
Lie doggo. This is not
an interrogation chamber.

The clock strikes again.
To pass the time,
you could try making up anagrams.
You could start with
ABSENCE and OBLIVION.

English Dictation

I

I woke up from my nap. The clock struck four.
I thought I'd go out on a City Tour.
I rang Reception. *Tours leave on the hour.*
I booked one: but the rain began to pour.

Still, better go. It made me think of our
debacle when we spent the day in Tours.
The trees were caked with ice and white as flour,
we got lost in the snow and found that dour

café – where waiters (and the wine) were sour.
The former looked askance at our amour –
quite right. It ended. Now I just devour
my guide books on another lonely tour.

II

The tour raised up my spirits from their trough.
We drank some wine. I met a man from Slough
who got us singing on the coach – although
I got fed up with 'Blossom on the Bough'.

But when I staggered back I felt quite rough.
I rang Reception, said: *I've got a cough.*
I need some pills and whiskey. She said: *Tough.*
I saw you coming in. You've had enough.

The Visit

They were acting out a tiresome folie à deux:
quarrelling as they arrived on the doorstep;
laughing and bickering over the drinks,
and then enacting some drama involving
mobile phones and third parties. We put up with it,
heavy with our married politeness and wry smiles,
though the charged air skewed the evening.
After they left (shouted farewells in the street,
the car revving up a storm) peace floated down
like feathers. But we felt dull. In bed
we recalled the days of our own capriciousness
and lay frowning, not at all at rest.

Holding Hands in the Movie Show

That first time: I was sixteen
and so was he. Difficult to know
who was more nervous. His hand
creeping over the armrest,
infinitesimally slow,
his shoulder touching mine, my heart
in a frenzy, the film a vague blur.

It was that sort of era –
or I was that sort of innocent.
But once the virginity of my palm was breached –
what delicious, eloquent hand-holdings:
passionate squeezes, delicate tracings
and strokings – furtive and illicit, perhaps,
or familiar, comforting.

Cut to half a century later,
to a grandchild, frightened
by a monster on the giant screen.
A head burrows into my shoulder,
a hand clutches mine, hanging on for dear life.
'Come on, be brave,' I murmur,
'it'll all be over soon.'

Metropolitan

The city's manic, but my Love is sane.
He likes the hustle – doesn't want to move.
My Love's not only urban, but urbane.

I'd leave tomorrow – gladly pack it in,
but he prefers the lamplight to the stars.
We lie in bed marooned inside the din.

He has to stay in reach of Waterloo.
He has to travel in the outside lane.
I tell him that I've grown to like it too.
That's love. You stack the loss against the gain.

Leviathan

Something has grown too big for the pond:
first the moorhens disappeared
then the ducks (corner-of-the-eye stuff,
nothing strictly attributable).
The Canada Geese stayed, but looked as if they knew
something they'd rather not think about.

A goat on the village green went mad overnight.
Then pensioners living nearby
started to peg out: heart attacks mostly
and always at Meals-on-Wheels time
(the body on the rug, the cartons emptied).
Alice Weevil went missing altogether.

A builder up a ladder, on his mobile,
didn't at first hear the flub of something
working its way up the rungs behind him.
'Quick Reg,' were his last words –
'get the pond drained – don't wait
for the Council – there's a huge, unbelievable –'

The R Word

I meant us to have a good life together:
trading words and gestures, achieving
some sort of closeness.
But it isn't working out like that.

Fragments of fruit fall, spurned
to the bottom of your cage
while you crouch, moping, in the corner.

Come on, it's not as if you ever lived
in a tree. The jungle
would be worse for you than SW13.

But the sky through the kitchen window seems
alien, and you flinch at the great predators,
roaring nose-to-tail on the flight path.

I flinch too. I realise I've taken on
what I always try to shirk.

Responsibility.

Escape

Of course she has to shout at him sometimes.
He hides his hearing aid in strange places:
in the fridge, in the teapot, under the carpet.

He follows her round, yet is no longer there
though some relic remains − intractable,
regressed, uttering an eternal chorus:
Where are you going? Where going?
Where? Where going?

They face each other across the hearth
in the evenings. One night
she slides low in her chair,
the evening paper swooping whitely
to the floor. At dawn he is still talking:
Where? Where are you going? Where going?

Ice Cream

It can't be the cornet I've just bought
from NICO'S ICE CREAM PARLOUR

and it isn't the unseasonable weather −
warm sun confounding the Christmas shoppers.

What is it? I rest my carrier bags
on a low wall outside Laura Ashley

and gaze at the market − customers hefting
melons; pigeons lined up on the roof of GAP,

stalls shining with aubergines, oranges, peppers,
vans unloading in organised chaos.

I take another mouthful of sweetness;
and euphoria turns to ecstasy, real and sharp.

You might not think it much of an epiphany.
You might think it's just a hormonal quirk.

I reach the bottom of the cornet
and even the last mouthful is succulent.

At Kill-Two-Birds

I am raising an army of mercenaries.
Any pensioner may apply – preference given
to the suicidal, the cranky, and those
who believe in sending a gunboat.

Much of the fighting will be technical
and sedentary; but a full sacrifice of casualties
is also planned. Medals will be freely awarded.
Enlist today. Bus with ramp collects.

Getting Out of Hand

Experimenting with virtual reality
she calls up a good-sized house, and in it she pops
Rupert Brooke, who comes out of his study
muttering octosyllabics and twisting
his inky fingers through his famous hair.

Remembering his penchant for anguished passion
she summons Charlotte Brontë – but something goes wrong
and it is Branwell who turns up, though it doesn't seem
to matter, and he falls into conversation with Rupert
about the rail service to Lulworth Cove.

They settle down for tea, and here comes Jane Austen
handing round the bread and butter. Cup in hand,
she leafs through a volume of diaries
found on the coffee table. Her eyes widen
and she drops the book with a nervous glance

over her shoulder, but there is no sign
of the author, for Joe Orton (if on the premises)
is engaged elsewhere. More figures
materialise, and surely someone will have to wash
the cups – though that doesn't look like a butler

limping in through the French windows, saturnine
and patrician, with a dangerous-looking hound in tow.
Someone who understands these animals is needed a.s.a.p.
and Conan Doyle springs to mind – being also qualified
to advise about the foot – but no, surely that's GBS

cycling bossily up through the garden
ready to sort everyone out, if he can make himself heard
above the shouting and barking. Now they're all
comparing something, and fragments of speech surface:
Missolonghi... mosquito... my best apple tree.

In the Palm of His Hand

I'm in love, I'm in love!
I know – I've cried Wolf before
but this time it's true.
I'm in for the full agony:
the contrived encounters;
the heart-shock of the doorbell;
the new meaning to life; the new lingerie.

How do I know it will get that far?
Because of his meaningful look
when he weighs my mange-tout, my pink fir apples.
Because he slips an extra nectarine into my basket.
Because on Tuesday he offered to deliver
to me personally, and he wrote my address
in the palm of his hand.

House Detective

My heartbeat imitates a castanet.
The sofa wears its dustsheet like a pall.
The house is manifestly empty. Yet
the floorboards creak across the empty hall.

The telephone is ringing by the bed.
The door's alarmed; the desk is quite distressed.
The empty car is singing by the kerb.
I think you've gone. I think it's for the best.

Home Truths

The three of us were having tea, I remember,
second cups and walnut cake going round
when my sister started singing the praises of Dorchester
and right away, taking another slice,
Dave went into raptures about the place –
Dorchester this, Dorchester that.
I said: *What are you talking about Dave?*
I'm sure we've never been there.
He just stirred his tea with a knowing smile.
I was put out, miffed. What call
had he got to gang up with my sister like that?
Some betrayals are so small
you can hardly put your finger on them
at the time.

The Aspirant

Don't look any further. If you want a victim,
take me. No matter how blunt the knife
or the words, choose me.

A spanner, an icicle, a scythe,
it's all the same: on a towpath
or in a bed at night.

I hang around auditions.
Most are trying for the murderer
but I covet the other role.

But it will go to someone else.
Someone wrong, but within reach,
A good girl, pillar of the local church.

Psychopaths with shards of glass,
let me pass without a glance.
Wallflower. I'm not invited for this dance.

The Upper Hand

I am frightened of this orderly.
Huge, with a black helmet of hair,
she slaps her broom round my bed
and, fixing me with a glittering eye,
intones something gnomic.

'Sorry?' I keep saying, and at last
the words fall into focus:
'Two pints of lager
and a packet of crisps.'
I laugh obediently, mime sudden sleep.

Now she is here again, smacking my locker,
bending over me, her face
close as an eye surgeon's.
'Are you with me,' she breathes,
'or with the Woolwich?'

'With you,' I say fervently.

At Madame Tussaud's

Seeing you in wax is a shock.
I hadn't realised you were here.

You stare glassily North-West,
with a slight curl of the lip.

The hand is excellently done, it reminds me
of certain intimacies, certain afternoons

in that room with the faulty light switch
and the purple sheets. We closed the blinds

and locked the doors. Love is so athletic –
a wine glass toppled in some amorous antic.

Afterwards there were drab days:
counsellors, consolers, a cold decline from your sun.

Here in wax you are all dignity and tailoring.
Thoughtfully I lean forward and start

to undress you, hardly noticing the faces
swivelling towards me. I work my way

through garment after garment, like a doctor
whose patient cannot help himself.

Elephants

Events loom towards you
blocking out the light like elephants –
births, deaths, weddings;
an appointment for root canal work.
A proposal. A diagnosis.

You've got to get past the date marked X
and then you're free until the next elephant
grows from a speck on the horizon
to a presence, towering between you
and the ordinary washing on the line.

Keeping on Top of Things

I want to be alone. But I have to see
the chiropodist, the dentist,
the car mechanic, the ear-syringer,
the roofer, the window cleaner,
and a man to cut back the creeper
which is forcing its way in
through the bedroom window.

Thank goodness I don't have to see
the manicurist, the otologist,
the arboriculturalist,
the reflexologist, the phrenologist
the hypnotherapist, the gynaecologist
the Chinese herbalist, or the psychiatrist –

at least not this week.

Next Please

Child power is overwhelming
the parents. Even the baby –
a prize marrow with a threatening eye –
is sucking the substance out of them;
and the toddlers are little Caligulas.

Grown-ups know their days
are numbered. Soon, with a dislocating yawn,
the children will swallow them,
leaving only shadows walking about
pretending to be sensible.

Mésalliance

I am divorcing my dog.
He never cared for me: we were
unsuited. His lickspittle allegiance
lies wetly elsewhere, his easy bonhomie
bounces over others.

I am barely acknowledged:
a mere opener of tins,
prison warder, valet.
In front of other dogs
he is insubordinate.

I mean to dispose of him
by auction. He suspects this:
snuffs and sighs as I batten down
for the evening. (A window left ajar
and he's gone.)

The back-up plan involves garden work.
He peers into my excavations
glaucous-eyed and curious,
but feints and weaves at my attempts
to catch and measure him.

Good Girl

She sleeps in the box room
in Mrs Johnson's house. She is twelve years old
but growing younger every day
away from home. Letters from her mother
are pale and creased with wear:
(*Be very good and when we get some petrol*
we'll come and see you. Tigger sends his love.)

Mr Rainey, the lodger, gives her a yellow smile
over the breakfast toast, while the others
rush off to their war-work.
Plump-fingered, silver-haired,
with something dark staining his waistcoat,
he divides his butter ration
into seven greasy morsels.

One morning she wakes to panic – a pool of blood
on the sheets, a fierce, gripping ache,
a hot wave of fear and shame.
She shuts herself in until Mrs J. comes home
and reassures her. *It's just growing up dear.*
Mysterious accessories, elaborate with elastic.
The sheets taken away with a tired sigh.

The bathroom is down a dim, narrow passage, a place
of awkward passings and pleasantries.
Coming out one day carrying something
shaming and private behind her back,
she comes face to face with Mr Rainey,
who puts a doughy hand on her shoulder.
I know what you'd like my dear. Ginger biscuits.

You must come and have tea in my room.
She runs to the kitchen stove, that temperamental
comforter and incinerator. She knows
she must accept: that is what
is meant by being good. So at four o'clock
he leans over her with his plate of biscuits.
His sardine breath shuts off the air.

Reunion

Walking round Kew with your mother
was tough. Why did you bring her?
Wasn't it difficult enough,
our meeting after twenty years apart?

Of course it was kind of her to point things out,
the statuary, the oriental wildfowl, the ice house,
the way the children were running about,
the way the weather was getting worse.

Lacunae? Not with your mother to take
advantage of each pause. Our swallowed words
lay heavy as rocks. Silence flew off
over the lake like a flock of birds.

Friend

(i.m. Margaret Budleigh)

Our friendship lasted more than forty years:
it wound between us like a golden thread
which never broke or loosened. You'll live on
in gestures we remember, times we shared.
Larkin was right: however we may grieve,
we know that what survives of us is love.

Musical Chairs

Whirling round we go,
though some of us don't like
the music. Some of us
don't even like the game, but
one by one we are spun off
into the dusk, where the laughter
echoes more faintly, the distant
fluted melodies modulate
to a minor key, the red balloons
and the yellow balloons
are losing their lustre
and the air thins out across the grass
to where the cliff shelves down
suddenly, the samphire clinging
to the crumbling edge. The sea below
is advancing and receding. It has
its own game, which is called
swallowing and scavenging.

Convalescence

Nothing could make her love him.
To cure himself of the pain
he hired a man (thin, hungry, voluble)
to speak ill of her from dawn to dusk.

Once a week the man stayed all night,
murmuring aspersions, sleeping in snatches
on a rattan chair. No change.
The man left, the obsession did not.

But one Tuesday, he awoke refreshed.
What was his beloved's name? It had slipped
his mind. He stood at the window, marvelling
at the oleander buds unfolding towards the sun.

FROM

Private Pleasures

(2007)

Under Your Skin

You may take it out on a lead;
you may give birth to it
you may be its child.

You will know which one it is
and it knows you.
It knows its power.

If it turns its back on you once
you say goodbye to sleep
all the live-long night.

Awakening

After a pint or two of Shires
the gas man is asleep in his van
on the common. The sun is hot on his face,
his feet are on the dashboard.

He dreams himself into a garden
with that lovely girl who does the weather
in figure-hugging turquoise...but his wife
is tip-tapping down the garden path towards them.

The tapping gets into his ear, like an earwig,
and he opens his eyes to a blurred face
outside the glass. It is Mrs Boiler-Problem
of Fifteen Park Drive.

Flakes of ash are clinging to her hair
and in the sooty darkness of her face, her eyes
are red and mad. She is mouthing words
no decent man wants to hear from a woman.

All the Kissing We Do Now

Not just the greeting and parting kisses,
but the maybe-this-person-could-give-me-a-contract
kiss; the what-was-her-name? kiss
the kiss electric, behind the coat rack.

The invasive kiss. The viral kiss.
The kiss that spreads something like wildfire
and keeps you awake half the night
for more reasons than you can shake a stick at.

Biography

When you were cut open,
the small bones of your lovers
were discovered inside you.
Shrunken skulls, tiny ankle bones,
femurs in miniature.

We arranged your prey with tweezers,
recognising a tooth here,
a digit there. What a big beast you were!
You could swallow a chorus line;
a sixth form; a pew-full of worshippers.

Now we are fighting over you,
stabbing each other with our spiky pens.
We want to eat you up.
It will make us famously potent.

Colouring Book

Here is the Common where she used to play.
Here are the trees she climbed and here is the path
twisted and shady.

There is the clover underneath her feet,
colour it pink. There are her new blue sandals,
see how they run.

Here is a stranger, following down the path
and into a glade. Did they meet in the glade?
Turn over the page.

Now they are out of sight. Is that a bird
or a cry that we hear? See how the sparrows
fly from the bush.

End Game

Those interminable games of chess...
I think it's the only reason he comes to see me.

    Those interminable games of chess.
    She always has the board out, waiting.

Generally I let him win. After all, he's come
from Chislehurst. It seems sad
to come so far for nothing
but tea and cake.

Sometimes I try to let her win,
but she's not much of a player.
At least she makes a decent pot
of Orange Pekoe.

I could be having a siesta
or catching up with my patchwork.
But that's just selfishness.

If I made an excuse next week,
I could get back to my notes on the Crimea.
But she'd miss me so much.

De-familiarisation

Now that his memory has gone,
his house is a treasure trove:
each drawer a surprise, each cupboard
a revelation.

Discovery is his obsession,
the ranks of photographs (a wife? a daughter?)
are his clues, studied at night,
unfamiliar by morning.

Daily he takes his walk
round the square. He knows his home
by its fig tree.

The house takes him back in, reveals its contents
to his astonished eye.

Out of My Mouth

I've heard all my opinions before
and I am tired of them.
They fall heavily out of my mouth
and lie around
like tiny, wizened children.

I don't blame you
for stamping on them.
We will do it together
and when the massacre is over
I will begin again –

my thoughts darting and colourful
as tropical birds.
You will hardly know me.
I'll hardly know myself.
So that's a start, anyway.

Background

When they met a second time
he persuaded her to come and see his garden –
which he'd mentioned on their first date.

The scene was one of chaos:
great scoops of earth flung about;
dank water in the depressions,

the whole edged by dark greenery
(Cypress, Leylandii, something spindly,
underplanted with Bugleweed).

In the centre, a small upright shed
crammed with planks of wood and tubing.
A foreground of buckets, lumps of stone,

something large and rusty. Mud.
He explained his plan: underground streams,
and a grotto half hidden by spotted laurels.

When will it be finished? she asked.
This (he calculated) *is year three,
but of course a garden is never quite finished.*

The soft wet ground sucked at her stilettoes
so despite herself
she had to grab hold of him.

Needs

I need to go shopping for mascara. He needs
to get to the pub before closing time.

You need to get out more
and put the past behind you.

She needs somewhere to sleep.
A lean-to would do for the night.

They need a square meal, or at least
a handful of maize.

She needs water. A cupful
could save her.

Advice

– so kindly meant,
so freely given –
so very often wrong.

A Change in the Weather

This is the rough you're given with the smooth.
This is the bad hand after all those aces.

This is the nerve that's jumping in your tooth:
This is the cold look after the embraces.

This is the something nasty in the sink.
This is the tentacle that grips you tightly.

This is the thought you cannot bear to think.
This is the way you think it, daily, nightly.

Loose Connections

It's hard to capture it on paper,
this elusive shape-shifting idea.
Yet if he can crystallise it,
hone it, make it succinct,

it could be his memorial –
a tiny atom of philosophy
handed down to posterity.
At any rate a footnote

to some greater work.
He takes his fountain pen
and a pad of lined paper,
and after seventeen minutes

(absently watching a magpie
trawling the roof gutter opposite)
he finds that he has written:
    Fix MOT. And find out
    how you get divorced.

Landscape with Figure

I can't reclaim the landscape of my mind.
Whichever way I turn, I see you there.
Friends say: 'A change of scene will help.' I find
that when the scene is changed, you reappear.

The figure in the distance on the beach,
her brown hair blowing, pointing out to sea –
however fast I run, she's out of reach
and when I call, she never turns to me.

I went back to our park. Remember how
we picnicked by the lake, and in the rain
we sheltered in the folly? Even now
I see you down each vista.
                   I'm in pain
The beauty of each landscape mocks my lack.
The sun shines cheerlessly. You won't come back.

Marrying the Car

He loved his car above everything,
polishing, cherishing – always
easing into it with a serious smile.
Giving it quality time.

Partners came and went. Hormones raged
in his blood, then unaccountably
drained away. Annoyingly
his last wife left with all his classical CDs.

Is it wrong to love a car?
Who can say. Some people love a house,
a song, a dog, a view.
Whatever helps you through the day will do.

Private Pleasures

Up to my elbows
in the juice
of a huge, ripe,
perfumed, unmanageable
mango,
I suddenly wonder
if I am being
watched.

Mango-moustached,
I hastily pull down
the blind.

Some things
are best enjoyed
in privacy.

Waving

Gazing from my bedroom window, admiring
the sun on the marigolds, I suddenly see
a woman at her own window opposite.
She is waving and waving.

I pull myself together. Is this an emergency?
Perhaps there is a burglar in the house,
or perhaps her husband has collapsed
against the bedroom door.

I wave back vigorously and reach for my binoculars.
And she is not waving at all, but cleaning her windows.
Her white cloth soars and plunges. Fortunately
she has not noticed me.

Song

When I walked back from your house last week
it seemed so mild for October.
The last of the light was gold
over the river, and when I passed the pond
five geese flew up in formation
banking low over the rooftops. Babies
were being wheeled home. The late flowers
in the front gardens were curiously brilliant –
the yellow evening primrose, blue love-in-a-mist;
a shower of white solanum, shimmering.
I was singing, under my breath,
the song we practised together
but I don't think anyone noticed.

Piccadilly in the Sunshine

The roadsweeping machine
is wheezing along past the commissionaires
in their Russian-prince uniforms

and its brushy little wheels buzz a path
through the polyglot strollers
with their bulging bags from Fortnum's;

and it weaves between the dark-suited men,
who are on their mobiles cutting serious deals
with Chicago or China or Chile,

though surely they should be saying

> Mother, it's such a lovely day
> why not ditch the Bridge
> and come and have tea at the Ritz?
> ...yes, profiteroles...
> and then we'll find some deck chairs;
> the park is so green and tempting today.

Then

That was the year, if you remember,
when the Last Request Bill was introduced.
Anyone over seventy was eligible.

The colours of the cubicles
were rich as Egypt; the couches
deeply sprung, the automatic sleep plungers
smooth and silent.

Some critics objected at first, do you recall?
But soon the self-propelled wheelchairs
were rolling up across the bumpy pavement –
later to be left outside,
empty but garlanded.

Universal Primer

When you set out to repaint a room,
those old diaries must be moved from the shelf.

First blow off the dust, then –
because you have them in your hand –

look up what you were doing this time
last year, and ten years ago,

and twenty. You'll probably need
a coffee, because of the dust

and to help you remember who it was
you were in love with – referred to

by those guarded initials – in 1978.
A newspaper cutting flies out

about a gynaecologist – and then one
heavily marked, about a window-cleaner:

surely neither was the mystery man, and yet...
some memory falteringly stirs. You read on

until dusk, then reach for the light switch.
A still life is sharply revealed

of sugar soap, white spirit and universal primer.

To Those People I've Annoyed by My Infatuations

First there was the boy with the hamster
who blushed and became monosyllabic;

then there was the music master
who ignored my notes;

was it the gynaecologist next?
Such men cultivate deafness;

and what about the psephologist?
My predilections were strange in those days.

Finally, that Austrian with no chin and a bow tie
who moved out of the district.

I'd like to apologise to you all
for the inconvenience caused

by my tears and sighs,
intrusions and lingering looks.

I am quite better now.

Page-turner

Yes, get straight on to the mystery woman
acrobat; or at any rate

the disgraceful Rites of Passage carry-ons.
Spare us the years of tranquillity

and for God's sake don't rabbit on
about how he reclaimed his garden season by season;

or that book on Baudelaire he kept failing to write.
We'd better examine the stormy marriages,

the break-outs from the rehab centre,
and most particularly, the rumours of incest.

Any serious student of psychology
needs to know about the incest.

Register his sad decline and don't skip the death –
though we'll certainly flinch at the pain and indignity.

The scenes at the funeral between
the mistresses makes a wry postscript –

and there we are: a life begun and ended
in a few hours, with hardly a hint of boredom.

Pack

No ducking stool,
no thumbscrew:

the hangman comes disguised
as a bloke –

with a camera
a million short words

and a heavy boot.
The victim survives long enough

for some sport.

The Speech

The voice goes on, a flat, unending drone.
When did he start? Today or yesterday?
Ring, ring, please ring, I urge my mobile phone.

The audience has aged and turned to stone.
A few slip out ('I'm off to the café').
The voice goes on, a flat, unending drone.

A pause. Our hopes are raised! But then a groan –
He carries on. I close my eyes and pray:
Ring, ring, please ring, I urge my mobile phone.

A woman faints: they dab her with Cologne.
She's better off unconscious I should say.
The voice goes on, a flat unending drone.

Why can't I leave? I've no will of my own.
Some astral force decrees that I must stay.
Ring, ring, please ring, I beg my mobile phone.
The voice goes on, a flat, unending drone.

Funeral Dog

Having a dog at your funeral
made all the difference.

The dog was quiet, snuff-coloured
and nondescript. We edged round
awkwardness by asking each other
his name, or bending over him
for a private moment of grief.

He seemed to know that this was his work
for the day. Afterwards, the rewards –
a wild run on the common, a biscuit
from the tin with the hollyhocks,
then the long stretched-out oblivion
of a job well done.

We Are So Many

In the bus, next to my knee, is a huge leg,
pale and bristly. It is part of a big man
in tiny shorts – a weight-lifter, perhaps
or someone from a genetically bulky family.

It sets me thinking about the problems of dissolution.
Can the crematoria cope with such solidity?
Otherwise, it's up to the earth to swallow us,
bus-fulls, train-loads, arenas of us –

and so much of the earth out of action
under patios and shopping malls.
At my gaze, the man shifts his leg uneasily,
and rings the bell. The doors hiss open for him.

Those Old Gods

They were always interfering – blowing over
ships, turning people into trees
on the merest whim.

The new generation are still at it:
setting off volcanoes, summoning
earthquakes, spreading plagues.

But something is missing.
It might be the knack of impersonation
or malicious playfulness.

Occasionally you catch an echo
of their old style: someone half-man, half-frog
trips you up on the bus,

or, in the half-light of dawn,
you catch your topiary bird
creeping back into its hedge

and settling impassively
on its root, the earth at its foot
barely disturbed.

Horticulture

Something in the compost bin
keeps trying to grow; raising
skinny white arms in pathetic supplication.

I turn the heap, crush and bury it,
but repeatedly it climbs up again,
refusing to rot.

Is there a metaphorical message in this –
am I meant to infer some truth
about Hope, Endurance and Rebirth?

Finally I give in, lift it out
and carefully plant it in the damp earth.
At once it keels over, staging a dramatic death.

In a Flash

You hand me a photograph, and in it,
your chin, with its five o'clock shadow
is a foil to the tender cheek
of your first-born.

But wait, it is only a moment since
you were the baby, lying on my bed,
staring curiously sideways,
as if getting to know the wallpaper,
or working out some plan.

You'll notice how quickly it all happens.
The photos fly in and out of the albums
like snow, like melting snow.

Why Didn't You Tell Me You Were Dead?

It was odd the way I found out:
coming across your name
on a plaque on that bench
(in Roman caps, HE LOVED THIS VIEW).

I thought of you –
never one to commend any view –
rebellious, cranky, funny;
touching my life then losing touch.

The years wound back
to you, leaning forward
either to kiss or to mock:
your beard vibrant with intent.

Not a bad idea, these markers
we invent, stretching our time
that single heartbeat more,
cairns, gravestones, pyramids,
plaques, words written
on a dark and shifting floor.

Finding a Leg
to Stand On

(2012)

Getting It Right

A dozen men have taken over the High Street
with cameras, equipment and badinage.
They wear wildly assorted headgear and scarves
and look too scruffy for surveyors.

We stand in the bus queue shivering and watching
as they manoeuvre their many cables.
They are chewing toffees from a big round tin
balanced on a camera. They are making a commercial.

Suddenly, one of them shouts 'Action'
and a girl in jeans comes out of a shop
and walks a few yards towards us.
But something is not quite perfect and she is sent back

again and again. We think about perfectibility
and when the bus comes we climb on with more care
than usual. Are we doing it with conviction?
Are we getting it right?

Finding a Leg to Stand On

It's like some Grimm fairytale:
One of us loses an eye, one an ear,
one of us a heart. Magic spells
don't work, so we take to bargaining:

an eye for an artery; a kidney
for a jug of blood. There are muggings.
Watch out – those of you with two good legs –
for the limping man who follows you home.

166

And if you have a sharp pair of eyes, take note
of the billowing of the curtain
at the window of your room,
as someone fumbles blindly towards you.

Save Your Breath

Faint last words waver up
from hospital pillows.

You will look after Jack won't you?
He needs combing for fleas morning and evening.

For God's sake make sure you pay off your mortgage
before you go skiving off to Goa;

and Angela, you must give up that dreadful man
he's no good for you at all.

The relatives nod and nod, leaning forward tenderly,
their fingers crossed behind their backs.

The Day of the Doors

Today I went to buy a travel pass
at Mr Patel's versatile shop, where
between the neatly arranged shelves
is a door I'd hardly noticed –
but today it was ajar,

and you could snatch a glimpse
of steep stone steps
between rough brick walls
down to a cellar piled with boxes
in apparent disorder.

I am not thinking Freud here: I am not
drawing parallels with Hades and Persephone
or mulling over Alice and the rabbit hole –
it simply seemed a coincidence
that on my way down to the Piccadilly Line

I passed a darkly-uniformed figure
who unlocked a dusty door
to an unkempt, much-cabled room –
no chance to have a good look before
he shut the door firmly behind him:

and in the department store,
as I passed a cloakroom and WC,
another anonymous door swung open, and inside
was a man with a wrench, scratching his head
and standing in a rather extensive pool of water.

Game On

Round the shiny table
men are sitting and refining
the Rules of War.

One is taking minutes
to make sure there are no mistakes
so that is all right then.

The Slope

Remember that plateau
where the days were infinite
and the streams ran slowly –

where the sun yawned itself
over the horizon and people
discussed which gloves to wear?

Now we run as we wake
and there's nowhere to stop
until it's time to sleep.

On the 10.15

They're as close as two people in a double bed
and his encroaching bulk makes her feel submissive
in an old-fashioned iron-your-shirts way.
His suit is expensive, as she can see from his sleeve
when she glances down from her *Guardian*; and he smells faintly
of soap and biscuits. Now he is on the phone:

'Yes, if you wouldn't mind feeding her…she wouldn't let me
touch her this morning. I left her something
in the conservatory but she's not eating much I'm afraid.'
With the lurching of the train, his elbow presses hers
and she believes it stays fractionally closer with each jolt.
His briefcase, plonked on the floor, nudges her ankle.

He folds his paper and starts to do the very crossword
which she is attempting and this makes her wonder
if they might make a future together. She closes her eyes
to picture their life: the country walks, the favourite
trattoria, the fireside exchanges ('Is that how you spell
Nietzsche? It doesn't fit in with Tamarind.')

But there is a sudden flurry at her elbow
and she opens her eyes to see him hurrying down the aisle
and crowding the door to get out at Basingstoke.

Stations

As he travels home on the Northern Line
he is reviewing his marriage.

When he used to tell her that he loved her
it was certainly true: but now the words –

though they still fulfil a useful and ceremonial
purpose – have lost some of their resonance,

as in *Barons Court* or *St John's Wood*
or the beautiful *Shepherd's Bush*.

My Lunch with Karl and Fleur

Come in old boy, come in.
How long is it? Five years? Eight?
Great to see you...dump your coat,
Fleur's in the kitchen.

The kitchen is bright, warm
with something poisonous in the air.
Fleur's kiss is rich in Sauvignon.
I take a chair.

Thanks Karl, whatever you're having ...
Yes, it's been an age.
Mid-Blair, it must have been?
You two weren't married then.

Karl and Fleur are keeping busy,
their backs turned to each other.
Fleur tears something off a bone.
Karl punishes garlic
with a kind of hammer.

*

Filling a silence, he says:
It's good to have you on your own
for a real heart-to-heart.

Fleur grimaces at me behind his back.
She refills my glass, asks me:
Still at the same address?
Living on your own?
We must make a fuss of you.

I'm sorry we're so late with lunch.
She puts a hand on my shoulder.

*

During a third awkward drink, my phone
vibrates. It's the dry cleaner with a spiel
about my trousers. I turn it off
and start apologising to Karl:

What a bugger it had to happen just now
but it's a bad fall, evidently.
They might have to operate,
and she's eighty-nine now, you know.

I take my coat with what I hope
is a grave expression, as I murmur:
We mustn't leave it so long next time.

The Lost Lover

I came to find you – came to find you twice,
at eight and then at ten. But not a trace –

although I caught the vestige of your scent
which in the circumstances was of scant

utility in working out the way
you'd left, and more important: why?

I guess that Jeremy is at the back
of this: you always answered to his beck

and call. I hate that man – his grizzled beard,
his paunch – the way he bullied you, and bored

the rest of us. Unhappily I roam
and search about for messages. The room

is bare and tidy, nothing out of place.
I shut the door. Once bitten, never twice.

November

My wife is at the ironing-board
and I am checking the racing results
when the heating comes on with a whoosh,
marking a change in the weather.

We don't comment, being in our own
cold zone. Hail peppers the windows;
leaves slap against the glass
and her iron spits as she observes

that I still haven't settled the bills
on my desk. I get up and turn off the TV
which has been babbling unnoticed,
though now I see it was serving a purpose.

Let's hope the weather improves
before we have to smile our way through Christmas.

The Body in the Library

is stiff with bitterness. A corpse again –
after thirty years in the business;
and today, as usual, it'll be all over for him
by the end of the opening credits.

He's got the looks, the attitude,
the charisma to be the Detective, or even
the Main Suspect; but how to project
from under a bloody sheet?

His heart is pounding from holding his breath,
his bullet hole is itching to distraction.
The director senses signs of rebellion:
Wish I had your job mate. Being dead's

a piece of cake. Can you do just a bit more
fixed-mad-stare when the sheet's pulled back?

Settling Down

Was it your third wife
or your fourth
you were so fond of?

The one with the short fuse
and the long, long hair
which she famously wound round your neck
during amorous play.

How she furnished us all
with smiles and whispers.

But well done, you –
settled as you are now
with that kindly lady
who never leaves you short of breath.

Too Many Metaphors

My subconscious staged a dream
last night, much embroidered with detail,
about a quest for a missing key
to a vast lorry, which I was to drive
on some epic journey.

But why take so much trouble?
Why not a simple message:
When you wake up, phone your mother
about the chest of drawers
and better say you'll pop in next week –
it's about time.

Reculer

He drew back, in order
to jump further.

Back and back he went
until, pleasantly tired,

he lay down under a baobab tree
thinking: that's enough exertion

for one life.

I Am Sending You This Present

because...

I am fond of you.
I am not fond of you, but I don't want you to know it.
I had two of them.
I feel guilty.

because...

I made it.
I need you to take me seriously.
my P.A. reminded me of the date.
I don't have the nerve to ignore Christmas.

because...

you're the only person I know who might use it.
it will smarten you up.
now you'll feel indebted to me.
I've had it for ages and I don't know what it is.

because...

there is something hidden inside it.
it's time you read something serious.
it will be company for you.
you gave me a present last year.

because...

it didn't suit me.
it doesn't cost much to feed.
you picked me up when I fell downstairs.
you always liked lilies when you were alive.

Late

Finding a hearse at rest outside my front door
is surprising. Looking for clues I furtively scan
the cards nestling in the flowers round the coffin...
Dear John... Our Wonderful Friend...

Now I see that the driver is on his mobile
and his course is obstructed by a van, out of which
a policeman steps, to semaphore a diversion.
There's been an accident on the road ahead. A fatality.

So, no way through to the crematorium from here,
and the road victim, though half way there already,
may not go direct but must first be carried
through the proper hushed procedures.

The hearse turns awkwardly
like a big, cumbersome beast,
then revs up and hurries off, to where
mourners regroup and frown over their watches.

Edited Out

(i.m. Elizabeth Bartlett)

Elizabeth, how you'd enjoy it
if you were here: and in a way you are
as we wait at the BBC to talk about you,
gazing at the cheerful scruffiness
of the men traversing the foyer on this humid day.

Here comes the producer, amiable and efficient,
her skirts swishing as we walk the corridors.
In the studio we listen to your own voice.
But as for reading from your letters – it's difficult
to by-pass the delicious indiscretions.

Sadly, there won't be another envelope
from you, with that tiny lucid script,
landing on the doormat. The cats
get edited out of the programme. Oh well,
it happens to us all, sooner or later.

Gait

Strangely, that's something I still miss:
your slow, measured stride. Even now
I'd try to copy it in case of crisis –
that thoughtful lope towards the fire or flood.

Of course you were panicking like the rest of us
but someone has to take the adult role.
I practise and practise – the cool head,
the steady hand, the firm,

what's-the-problem-here stroll
to the edge of the abyss.

Fever

The window in my bedroom is ajar
and the rattle of the builders' ladders
against the house next door, drowns
the rattle of the aspirin in its bottle,
and the faint sussuration
of the sparkling water in the glass.

The builders are in high spirits.
Jokes and badinage fly
up and down the ladders.
But now they turn on the electric drill
which vibrates the bed, and reminds me
that the top of Beethoven's head

was sawn off, after death –
a process described to me
by a man in a deerstalker
on one of those interminable train journeys,
where the trolley rattles its bottles
up and down the aisles

dispensing bitter coffee
and cake so hermetically sealed
you have to take a saw to open it,
and he compares the Beethoven operation
to the opening up of Shelley for his heart
using thumbnail sketches and diagrams – also

instruments, which he draws from his pocket –
and it is hot, hot, in this noisy train
but now the door is opening
and a wave of air stirs the blue curtains,
teases the sheets, and lifts
the petals of the flowers by my bed.

Telepathy

Think of an object,
she said to her husband,
write it down secretly
and I'll try to draw it.

He thought of a bed
but she drew an elephant.

That explains a lot, he sighed.

Blu-tack

When you planned it two weeks ago
it seemed a good idea.
Friends to supper! A to meet B;
C to be impressed by your Thai cooking;
D because he needs a square meal,
X and Y to lend a frisson of transgression.

Now, waiting for the bell to ring,
you are in hermit mode.
Standing amongst the terrible complications
of the kitchen, you long for
a remote cave, a quiet piece of bread.
To escape, in fact, through the garden gate.

You scribble a note for the front door:
SO SORRY – DOMESTIC CRISIS – BACK TOMORROW.
But where is the Blu-tack? You up-end the drawer
and as you find it, the doorbell rings.

Cat haiku

Walking back from the vet
my basket empty now.
The sadness of things.

Only Connect

Roused from my book
by feeling a hand on my arm
I register that an elderly Chinese lady
has sat down beside me in the crowded bus
and is talking to me eloquently
in Chinese, accenting certain points
by pinching my sleeve
and looking expressively into my face.

She talks to me for the length
of several bus stops
and I listen carefully
but no single word is familiar.
Yet I feel I should respond, and
at a tiny break in her discourse, I try:
Are you going into Kingston to shop?

While she replies – or at any rate
resumes her monologue –
I have a chance to notice
that she is tiny, carefully dressed
in dark clothes, and with a small
sparkling brooch at her throat.
We journey on, two people
hopelessly attempting a dialogue.

I interrupt her to ask
if she is shopping with a friend,
for I am nervous that she may
follow me through department stores
pulling at my sleeve and offering
advice. She might want
to come into the changing rooms
while I try on blouses.

But suddenly she falls silent
as if I'd spoken out of turn
or trespassed on some Chinese taboo.
We are at the end of the line,
and as we step on to the pavement
I am happy to see her reclaimed
by an elderly oriental man, and,
arm in arm, they smilingly disappear.

Was it all a practical joke?
Perhaps she often sits next to people
on public transport and teases them
by reciting, say, *Hamlet* in Chinese.
Or perhaps some releasing confession
has been taking place. If so,
we both know that her secret
will be safe with me.

Witness

Feeling under constant observation
must be like believing one is watched by God
though in my case the observer
is the father of my future neighbour.

He is scraping the inside of the sash windows
opposite my kitchen. It is taking him weeks
for unlike some more celestial being
he only works at weekends. It is Sunday

and I am washing up with brio, also my surfaces
are immaculate. Not for me the licked knife
or that indelicate fit of scratching
which the solitary life can so easily accommodate.

Aunt Maud and the Battle of Britain

It was all glitter and shine at Aunt Maud's,
where I'd been sent for safety.
First, the great marcasite ring
on the hand she held out to me (a present,
she told me later, from her third pilot)

then the silver box of *Balkan Sobranie*
on the glass coffee-table. I soon got used
to the satin shimmer of her peachy underwear –
often in evidence during the heat; and the shine
on the collar of her belligerent Jack Russell.

We lay in the garden and craned up at the bright sky
where tiny glinting Spitfires darted and swerved in battle,
sometimes exploding in a flash of orange
and spiralling down
into the green fields of Buckinghamshire.

Retirement 1948

My father, in his Pooterish phase,
has embarked on the Eustace Miles Grass Diet,
and the book lies open in the kitchen
near the small pile of grass cuttings
which he has filched from the bowling green.

The last hobby had been Cooking with Oats
(unsuccessful) and before that
Life Drawing – where he dashed off
some surprisingly frank studies,
incurring my mother's scandalised

disapproval. She was pleased
when he started to teach himself to type,
shut away in the dining room with a hired
machine. Lonely but determined,
he struggled with QWERTY until

caffeine hunger drove him back
(for tea and a *Player's Navy Cut*)
to the kitchen, and that is where
I remember him now, riffling through
the day's grass cuttings,

which Eustace assured us would promote
health, vigour and – he hinted – immortality.

I Am My Son's Fourth Child

The other three are off his hands
but now he has acquired this fourth,

who falls over, loses keys, socks,
and the thread of the argument;

has phases of monomania
and responds poorly to suggestion.

Boarding out is a possibility:
expensive, but worth every penny.

Ceremony

When I arrive, my mother looks up at me
anxiously, as though suspecting impersonation.
I dreamt I didn't know you, she says.

I spread my new dress over the bed
for her to look at and she strokes the fabric –
checking the seams and the set of the sleeves,

twisting a scrap between her fingers
to see if it creases, lifting it up
to the light from the window.

Oh yes, it's got – she hesitates,
tapping the table – *it's got ceremony.*
I like the word, with its hint of fullness and colour.

Now she is trying to find a needle –
for a dressmaker knows that a stitch
here or there is usually needed
to make everything absolutely right.

Some Rejections Are Unexpected

Sitting by my mother's bed
in her nursing home, I prepared
for a long, final watch as she drifted in and out
of consciousness; but after a while
she stirred, opened her eyes
and spoke faintly: *Go home now*, she said.

Go home? But this was meant to be
the deathbed event for which I had steadied myself –
the final, tearful, hand-holding scene.

But obviously, dying can involve concentrated effort
and some people like to work through it
undisturbed. I think I'd be the same.
At least that's what I told myself
as I gathered my things together, stooped
to kiss her, and walked out
through the burgeoning garden.

Spring Through the Looking-glass

In Spring the dress rails are blooming
with pink linen, flowered décolletage,
slippery wisps of silk. We feast on them
with eyes watering from the wind.
We finger them with our woolly gloves.
Our bodies yearn for them, inside our wrappings
of sweaters, scarves, tights, complicated layers
of elasticated underwear. Hats.

We imagine ourselves polished, tanned,
minimal in ice cream colours – hold up
skimpy cottons in front of the long mirrors
but our winter skin is tortoise-like,
or like something recently dug up.
It's no use. It would take hours to undress,
so we hurry up to the coffee shop, in case
they might, yet again, run out of doughnuts.

Plants Behaving Badly

The vines have gone mad after the storm.
Their tendrils whip through suburban trellises
lashing out at passers-by. They worm
through pockets, plackets, crevices.
It must have been something in the rain.

Speedy as snakes, they slither
through car windows, latch on to ears
wrists, dreadlocks. No one knows
what they want. No one dares
to call for secateurs.

Feeding Your Cat

The recalcitrant lock
the gloomy hall
the unfamiliar creakings
and sussurations,
the bored letters, waiting
to be picked up.

The stink of lilies
drooping in their huge vase
in a ring of unlatched petals.
How suddenly you left for –
where was it? Los Angeles?

I can't find the cat.
But startlingly, she leaps out
like a trouper from
behind a curtain, tail up,
with an expression I read as:
About bloody time too.

When I bend over her saucer
she bites my hand. It might be
a love bite, and I decide to give her
the benefit of the doubt.

'O Tell Me the Truth'

(after Auden)

Will it start with a vague apprehension?
Will it come as a pain in the chest –
or a place which we don't like to mention?
Will it be introduced by a test?

Will you wake up together one morning
because it's crept into the house?
Will it strike like a snake without warning?
Or play like a cat with a mouse?

Will it come with a wave in the ocean
or a leap, or a handful of pills?
Will it cause a tremendous commotion
or end with that soft air that kills?

Can you fool it by blaming your mother
or offering payment in lieu?
Please find out one way or another
and tell me the truth when you do.

Quest

You often mentioned it in your letters:
'Next time I come to stay with you we'll go
to X' (you had the tourist leaflet, the map)

but you were never quite well enough
for the journey, so X receded
like some much-mentioned Utopia,

some Ithaka, and yet
an everyday paradise, tricked out
with shopping malls, markets,

and little shops which might supply
(your Holy Grail) unusual razors
or parts for your obsolescent motor.

But anyway, death spared you
disillusion: you never knew
the seamier side of X –

the gritty, windswept bus station,
the litter blowing round the market place,
the baffling one-way system,

and after all, where you are
is so much pleasanter – so green,
so branchy, so rich in birds.